Max Stirner Bibliography

One Hundred Years of Criticism

Trevor Blake

Cover by Matt Lawrence
mattlawrencecreative.com

First Printing: 2016
Revision of May 2016

[Stirner, Max] Blake, Trevor
[English]
Max Stirner Bibliography / Trevor Blake.
ISBN 978-1-944651-01-5
    1. Philosophy
    2. Reference Books
Max Stirner (1806 - 1856); Trevor Blake

The author welcomes corrections and additions...

Letters:
P. O. Box 2321
Portland, OR 97208-2321 USA

Packages:
715 NW Hoyt Street #2321
Portland OR 97208-2321 USA

ovo127.com

127 House – At each turn of its thought, society will find us waiting.

CONTENTS

INTRODUCTION

Max Stirner was born in 1806 in Bayreuth, Bavaria. In 1826 he attended the University of Berlin and studied under Georg Hegel. He also attended the University of Erlangen and was a contemporary of Ludwig Feuerbach. In 1841 he socialized at a wine bar with Bruno Bauer, Friedrich Engels, Karl Marx and Arnold Ruge in a group called *Die Freien* (The Free). Stirner wrote *Kunst und Religion* (Art and Religion) in 1842. In 1845 he wrote *Der Einzige und sein Eigentum* (The Ego and Its Own), the foundation document of egoism. Stirner wrote *Recensenten Stirners* (Stirner's Critics) in 1845, *Die Philosophischen Reactionäre* (The Philosophical Reactionaries) in 1847 and *Geschichte der Reaction* (History of Reaction) in 1851. He translated *The Wealth of Nations* by Adam Smith and *Traite d'Economie Politique* by Jean-Baptiste Say into German. Max Stirner died in Berlin, Prussia in 1856 at the age of 49.

This book is a bibliography of Max Stirner in print from 1845 to 1945, from the publication of *The Ego and Its Own* to a century after. Entries are arranged chronologically and are followed by an excerpt from the source documents. Original spelling is retained but punctuation has been standardized. Essays on Stirner are included after the bibliography. The documents cited here were gathered over many years from used and rare booksellers and from the Internet. This bibliography was compiled between 2012 and 2016. The author welcomes additional information and corrections.

Nothing is more to me than myself, but it is the hope of the author that the reader will benefit from learning more about Max Stirner and his remarkable book *The Ego and Its Own*.

Trevor Blake
Portland, Oregon USA
May 2016

BIBLIOGRAPHY

Norddeutsche Blätter

Band II, IX. Heft. Berlin (March 1845) S. 1-34

Book review of *Der Einzige und sein Eigenthum* by Max Stirner. Book review by Szeliga (also known as Franz Zychlin von Zychlinski).

Die Kritik characterisirt und entwickelt sich selbst, indem sie ihren Gegenstand characterisirt und sich entwickeln läßt. Der *Einzige* gibt ihr die Gelegenheit zu einer neuen That der Selbstvervollkommnung. Sie wird zunächst dem Lebenslauf des Einzigen folgen. Der *Einzige* giebt sich sogleich zu erkennen als der, welcher seine Sache auf Nichts gestellt hat. Ich hab meine Sach' auf Nichts gestellt, sagt er, auf Nichts als auf Mich, auf Mich, der Ich da Nichts von allem Andern, der Ich mein Alles, der Ich der *Einzige* bin. Ich habe die glänzendsten Beispiele vor Augen, daß der Egoist am Besten fährt: Ich sehe, daß jener Sultan Keinen duldet, der es wagte, nicht der Seine zu sein Jeden in den Kerker wirft, der Seinem (des Sultan's) Egoismus sich entziehen will, daß er Sich Alles in Allem, Sich der Einzige ist. Ich sehe ferner den einträglichen Egoismus des Volks, das sich von ergebenen Patrioten schützen diese im blutigen Kampfe oder im Kampf mit Hunger und Noth fallen läßt und durch den Dünger ihrer Leichen ein blühendes Volk wird. Ich sehe ferner, daß die Wahrheit die Freiheit, die Humanität, die Gerechtigkeit nichts anderes begehren, als daß man sich für sie enthusiasmiren ihnen, ihrer Sache dienen soll.

Die Letzten Philosophen by Moses Hess

Darmstadt: C. W. Leske [June] 1845

Book-length appreciation of Max Stirner.

> Wer nicht bereits die geschichtliche Entwickelung des Christenthums und der deutschen Philosophie hinter sich hat, könnte meinen, die in jüngster Zeit von den deutschen Philosophen veröffentlichten Schriften seien auf Anstiften der Reaction herausgegeben. - Gelang es mir doch kaum, diese Ansicht einem Manne, der früher selbst an der Spitze der Junghegelianer stand, in Bezug auf Bruno Bauer auszureden. Und doch waren damals die Bauer'schen Schriften noch weit von der "Consequenz" seiner spätern entfernt, geschweige denn, daß sie den Cynismus der neulich von Stirner herausgegebenen Schrift erreicht hätten.) Trotz alle dem ist es dennoch wahr, daß weder Bruno Bauer, noch Stirner sich jemals irgend wie von Außen bestimmen ließen.

Wigand's Vierteljahrsschrift

Band II, [July] 1845, S. 193-205

"Über das 'Wesen des Christentums' in Beziehung auf den *Einzigen und sein Eigentum*" by Anonymous (also known as Ludwig Feuerbach).

Der Gedanke der Gattung in diesem Sinne ist für da einzelne Individuum - in Jedem ist ein Einzelner - ein notwendiger, unentbehrlicher. "Wir sind allzumal vollkommen", sagt der *Einzige* [...] wahr und schön; aber gleichwohl fühlen wir uns beschränkt und unvollkommen, weil wir uns notwendig notwendig, denn wir sind nun ein mal reflektierende Wesen nicht nur mit andern vergleichen, sondern auch mit uns selbst, indem wir das, was wir geworden sind, mit dem, was wir werden konnten, unter andern Verhältnissen vielleicht wirklich geworden wären zusammenhalten. Wir fühlen uns aber nicht nur moralisch wir fühlen uns selbst auch sinnlich, räumlich und zeitlich beschränkt; wir, diese Individuen, sind ja nur an diesen bestimmten Orte, in dieser beschränkten, erbärmlichen Zeit. Wo sollen wir uns nun von diesem Beschränktheitsgefühl erlosen, wenn nicht in dem Gedanken der unbeschränkten Gattung, d.h. in dem Gedanken anderer Menschen, anderer Orte, anderer glücklicherer Zeiten Wer die Gattung daher nicht an die Stelle der Gottheit setzt, der lässt in dem Individuum eine Lücke, die sich notwendig wieder durch die Vorstellung eines Gottes, d.h. des personifizierten Wesens der Gattung, ausfüllt. Nur die Gattung ist imstande, die Gottheit, die Religion aufzuheben und zugleich zu ersetzen. Keine Religion haben, heisst: nur an sich selbst denken; Religion haben an andere denken. Und diese Religion ist die allein bleibende, wenigstens solange, als nicht ein "einziger Mensch nur auf Erden ist; denn sowie wir nur zwei Menschen, wie Mann und Weib, haben, so haben wir auch schon Religion. Zwei, Unterschied, ist der Ursprung der Religion das Du der Gott des Ich, denn ich bin nicht ohne Dich; ich hänge vom Du ab; kein Du - kein Ich.

Wigand's Vierteljahrsschrift

Dritter Band [September] 1845, S. 86-146

"Charakteristik Ludwig Feuerbachs" by Anonymous (also known as Bruno Bauer).

Der Kritiker geht unaufhaltsam, siegesgewiß und siegreich seines Weges. Man verläumdet ihn: er lächelt. Man verketzert ihn: er lächelt. Die alte Welt macht sich auf in einem Kreuzzuge gegen ihn: er lächelt. - Max Stirner ist der Anführer und Heerführer der Kreuzfahrer. Zugleich der Tüchtigste und Tapferste von allen Kämpfern. Vor dem Einzigen und seinem Eigenthume fällt der politisch Liberale, der den Eigenwillen brechen will und der sociale Liberale, der das Eigenthum zerstören will. Sie fallen vor dem kritischen Messer des Einzigen. Allein der kritisch Liberale, der nach der Meinung des Einzigen dem Menschen seinen Egoismus, seine Eigenheit nehmen will - der will nicht fallen vor der Kritik, weil er selber der Kritiker ist. Was macht der Einzige mit ihm? Nein, ruft er, es wird nichts daraus. Meine Eigenheit gehört mir. Die behalte ich; die darfst und sollst du mir nicht nehmen, Kritiker.

BLAKE

Leipziger Revue

Nr. 3 1847

"Moderne Sophisten" by Kuno Fischer.

In der Entwicklung des denkenden Geistes ist das sophis
tische Selbstbewußtsein stets der eonsequente Gegenstol
die idealistische Spcculation und im Interesse de'
endlichen Subjcctivität die Reaetion gegen den dominiren
den Gedanken gewesen Die Sophistik ist der philosophi
sche Schalk der dem enthusiastischen Drange des Denken
die Härte des Individuums entgegensetzt und das Subjee
mit seinen Trieben und dem Idealismus des Gedanken
entzieht wo Faust zu geht triumphirt Mephisto [...] Ist e
nun nach dieser Begründung des absoluten Egoismus wirk
lich Ernst mit der Gedanken und Voraussetzungs loflgke
des Einzigen ist Stirner und sein Einziger hiernach wirk
lich der unumstößliche Herr jeder natürlichen und geisti
gen Macht und ist in der That jeder Gedanke jedes Dogm
in das "schöpferische Nichts" zurückgegangen aus dem e
wie eine illusorische Seifenblase aufgestiegen ist?

Revue Philosophique de la France et de l'Étranger

T. 3 (January to June 1877), pp. 609-626

"Léon Dumont Et Son Œuvre Philosophique" by J. Delbœuf.

> A l'anthropolatrie de L. Feuerbach succeda immediatement l'autolatrie de Max Stirner, et le developpement de l'idee hegelienne conduiset la science philosophique en plein materialisme.

Briefwechsel und Tagenbuchblatter aus den Jahren 1825 - 1880 by Arnold Ruges

Berlin: Weidmannsche Buchhandlung 1886.

The published diaries of Arnold Ruges.

> Ein sehr geistreiches Buch ist: *Der Einzige und sein Eigenthum* von Stirner bei Wigand. Die Schriftsteller werden immer fühner, die 2 heiste der Deutch - frz. Jahrbücher sind lange furpassirt durch heines Gedichte und durch Stirners Buch, die 2 bedeutendsten Erscheinungen der lessten Zeit [...] Hössler hat Ihnen Stirners Untwort gebracht. Der Mohr ist unzurechnungsfähig. Es ist gewiss gut, wenn Sie Stirner in einem Briese antworten und ihn über seine hauptdummheit noch einmal gründlich stolpern lassen.

The Philosophical Review

Vol. 1, No. 1 (January 1892), pp. iii-ix

"Contents of Volume I" cites *Max Stirner und Friedrich Nietsche, Erscheinungen des modernen Geistesund das Wesendes Alensche* by Robert Schellwien (Leipzig: Verlag von C. E. M. Pfeffer, 1892). Uncredited.

Revue Philosophique de la France et de l'Étranger

T. 34 (July to December 1892), pp. 331- 335

Book review of *Max Stirner und Friedrich Nietzsche, Erscheinungen des modernen geistes, und das Wesen des menschen* by Robert Schellwien (Leipzig: Pleffer 1892). Book review by Lucien Arréat

> L'opuscule de M. R. S. offreun réel intérêt, à cause d'abord des deux personnages qu'il met en scène, Max Stirner et Friedrich Nietzsche. Ces philosophes sont peu connus chez nous malgré les richesses paradoxales et le mérite littéraire qui ont pu donner, en Allemagne, de la saveur à leurs écrits. M. R. S. essaye, en une courte introduction, de marquer leur place dans l'histoire de la pensée moderne, et il tente d'expliquer cette histoire par l'effort constant de l'homme à construireune philosophie individualiste, dont Stirner et Nietzsche seraient les prophètes audacieux, et que lui-même représenterait à son tour, d'une autre manière, en échappant aux contradictions qu'il leur reproche.

The Monist

Vol. 3, No. 1 (October 1892)

"Contents of Volume III" cites *Max Stirner und Friedrich Nietsche, Erscheinungen des modernen Geistesund das Wesendes Alensche* by Robert Schellwien (Leipzig: Verlag von C. E. M. Pfeffer, 1892). Uncredited.

The Philosophical Review

Vol. 1, No. 6 (November 1892), pp. 661-662

Book review of *Max Stirner und Friedrich Nietzsche, Erscheinungen des Modernen Geistes, und das Wesen des Menschen* by Robert Schellwien. Book review by Ernest Albee.

> The author's fundamental assumption is that modern thought is essentially individualistic. The first two chapters of the book are on Max Stirner and on Friedrich Nietzsche respectively, two notable exponents of absolute individualism, whose views are presented as being the best, because the most consequent, examples of this individualistic tendency, which the author finds so alarmingly prevalent. The chapter on Stirner is wholly expository; that on Nietzsche, critical as well.

Revue Historique

T. 53, Fasc. 2 (1893), pp. 404-437

Citation of *Recueils Periodiques et Societes Savantes, Revue politique et litteraire (Review bleue) 1893*. Uncredited.

> No 15. Jean Thorel. Les peres de l'anarchisme: Bakou nine, Stirner, Nietzsche.

Mind, New Series

Vol. 2, No. 5 (January 1893), pp. i-viii

Book review of *Max Stirner und Friedrich Nietsche, Erscheinungen des modernen Geistesund das Wesendes Alensche* by Robert Schellwien (Leipzig: Verlag von C. E. M. Pfeffer, 1892). Review uncredited.

> This pamphlet is a vigorous protest against the naturalism and atomistic individualism of the age. Max Stirner and F Nietzsche are selected for special examination becaus they exhibit this tendency in the most conspicuous and un restricted way. Both proclaim the self-realisation of the in dividual to be the sole good and sole reality. Truth an right inasmuch as they impose restraint on the individua are regarded by them as mere chimeras. Now the autho while admitting that such views are absurd, maintains tha they are the logical expression of the stream of tendency c our time. In Baconian language they are *Instances Free and Predominant* of the general drift of thought. A mo important manifestation of this prevailing tendency is th pretension of natural science to afford an ultimate and ade quate account of reality. Nearly two-thirds of Mr. Schel wien's work is occupied by a trenchant criticism of th

common naturalistic assumptions. The arguments which he urges are in the main Hegelian, and the mode in which they are treated reminds us of Green and Caird. It is shown that knowledge and the pursuit of moral ideals are impossible to an individual who is merely an individual. They are possible only through the self-realisation in the individual of the one identical creative activity in and through which all things are. Unlike the English Neo-Hegelians, Mr. Schellwien habitually names this absolute activity *will* not *thought*. But, so far as the present book is concerned, this difference does not appear to be much more than verbal.

The Monist

Vol. 3, No. 2 (January 1893), pp. 306-312

Book review of *Max Stirner und Friedrich Nietzsche. Erscheinungen des modernen Geistes und das Wesen des Menschen* by Robert Schellwien (Leipsig: C. E. M. Pfeffer 1892). Review by KPC.

> Individualism is the spirit of the age, and among all the
> champions of individualism the most original, the most
> consistent, the boldest, are perhaps Max Stirner and
> Friedrich Nietzsche. Robert Schellwien, in sketching their
> views in great outlines, partly admires these courageous
> thinkers who dare to draw the consequences of their prin-
> ciples to the very last even though they will appear absurd
> to the world, partly censures the rashness with which they
> arrive at, and the superciliousness with which they some-
> times state, their opinions. Upon the whole the author suc-
> ceeds in impressing the reader that there is in these two pe-
> culiar geniuses a gigantic strength, and that their views of
> truth, morality, and justice deserve a greater attention than
> they have received. The reviewer is no admirer of either
> Stirner or Nietzsche; he believes nevertheless that a careful
> analysis of their erratic minds and lives will be very in-
> structive. It will be first of pathological and then even of
> more than pathological interest. The actual objective value
> of the ideals truth, morality, and justice, will be best illus-
> trated by showing all the consequences of a consistent in-
> dividualism. We hope that this pamphlet will grow into a
> more comprehensive work; and in that case we should ad-
> vise the author to add short biographies of his heroes.

Revue de Métaphysique et de Morale

T. 1, No. 2 (March 1893), pp. 202-207

"Periodiques Allemands." Uncredited.

> Zeitaschrift fur exakte Philosophie. Band XIX, Heft 3. R. Schelwein, Max Stirner und Fr. Nietzsche (id).

Revue Philosophique de la France et de l'Étranger, Deuxième Table Générale Des Matières: Contenues Dans Les Années 1888 A 1895

(1895), pp. 1-29

"Table Alphabétique Des Noms D'auteurs and Table Analytique Des Matières" by J. Clavière.

> Schellwein. Stirner et Nietzsche, 1892, II, 331.

Revue Philosophique de la France et de l'Étranger

T. 41 (January to June 1896), pp. 463-464

Book review of *Friedrich Nietzsche, ein kampfer gegen seine zeit* by Rudolf Steiner (Weimar: E. Felber 1895). Review by L. Arréat.

> M. Steiner [sic] a su parler de Nietzsche, apres beaucoup d'autres, d'une maniere interessante, et il a le merite de la faire brievement.

The Philosophical Review

Vol. 5, No. 4 (July 1896), pp. 443-444

Book review of *Allgemeinheit und Einheit des Sittlichen Bewusstseins* by Willhelm Schneider (Köln: J. P. Bachem 1895). Review by Frank Chapman Sharp.

> The thesis which the author has set out to prove is the familiar one, that the ethical codes of all peoples are in complete agreement as far as fundamental principles are concerned, and that the well-known divergence in moral judgments and in customs supposed to mirror such judgment is confined, wherever verifiable as fact, to subordinate details or to the application of the principles to the changing conditions of life. This established, our author hopes t have taken the ground from under the feet of the "*gottlos und jenseitslose, auf rein irdische und fleischliche Grundsätze gestützte Sittlichkeit*," represented by such boon companions as Höffding, Max Stirner, Paulsen, Nietzsche, an Wundt.

Revue Philosophique de la France et de l'Étranger

T. 42 (July to December 1896), pp. 210 - 213

Book review of *Der Geist der neueren Philosophie* by Robert Schellwien (Leipzig: A. Janssen 1896). Review by L. Arréat.

> Viennent maintenant L. Feuerbach, qui achève le mouve-ment tournantversle naturalisme, la nature, ensomme, était le principe, et l'esprit le résultat), et prend pied dans la "sensibilité;" avec lui, la vérité n'est plus qu'un produit de la vie collective; Max Stirner, qui repousse l'humanisme de Feuerbach et de Bruno Bauer et fait de l'homme-indi-vidu le commencement et la fin de la philosophie; Schopenhauer, qui abandonne décidément le réalisme ob-jectif et revient chercher dans l'homme intérieur le quelque chose de primordial et d'essentiel, antérieur à toute appari-tion dans le temps, l'espace et la causalité, qui sera la volonté.

The English Historical Review

Vol. 11, No. 44 (October 1896), pp. 751-752

Book review of *De Staatsleer van Hegel en hare toepassing* by Willem Carel Adrien Baron van Vredenburch (Utrecht: P. D. Boer 1896). Review by W. Hastie.

> The principle of realized freedom in the State, elaborated
> in his own way by Hegel, has indeed a certain obvious
> affinity with the historical character and movement of the
> political life of Holland; but Dutch thinkers, trained in the
> more lucid French and English schools, have not found
> themselves at home in its expression, and they have "let
> the Hegelian cup pass by." Nor will this academic thesis,
> intelligent and painstaking though it may be, quicken any
> fresh enthusiasm either in Holland or elsewhere for its
> subject. It removes none of the difficulties of Hegel's the-
> ory - its Lesbian criterion of right, its topsy-turvy inversion
> into unbridled individualism by Max Stirner on the one
> hand and its resolution into thoroughgoing socialism by
> Lassalle on the other, its covert vindication of "the Prus-
> sian system of 1821," dwelt upon by Haym and others, its
> often strained abstract formalism, and its comparative
> sterility both as regards subsequent political thought and
> its influence on special historical research.

The Monist

Vol. 7, No. 3 (April 1897), pp. 380-414

"The Conflict of Races, Classes, and Societies" by
G. Fiamingo.

> Social relations find their basis and their *raison d'etre* in
> the individual, but when individualism is pushed to the ex-
> treme of Max Stirner, of Frederic Nietzsche, or R. Schell-
> wein it is unsustainable. "*Ich singe, weil ich ein Sänger
> bin. Euch aber gebrauche ich da her, weil ich Ohren
> brauche. - Ich hab mein Sach' auf Nichts gestellt.*" Or as
> another writer says: "The ego, the single existing individu-
> al man, is the only thing. Outside of myself, there is noth-
> ing. The ego, as religion affirms of deity, is inexpressible,
> and it is perfect since it is at every moment all that it can
> be. More it cannot be, nor has it need of being. Every other
> being or thing is my property in so far as I have the power
> to appropriate it, and in so far as I wish it." Now this is
> blind individualism. As a matter of fact, the individual
> finds it useful to associate his efforts with those of other
> individuals in order that he may obtain in the labor of pro-
> duction a greater quantity of goods.

American Journal of Sociology

Vol. 2, No. 6 (May 1897), pp. 792-800

"The Present Status of Sociology in Germany III" by
O. Thon.

A sign of the relation between socialism and individualism
appears in the fact that wherever the former is found, the
latter immediately shows itself in force. In Germany
where socialism is advancing toward victory, individualistic tendencies of every sort are more and more vigorous.
Fifty years ago, when socialism was not so strong, and had
less place in the consciousness of the population, Max
Stirner's powerful book, *Der Einzige und sein Eigenthum*,
attracted little notice. On the other hand Friedrich Nietzsche has given our own time a violent electric shock. His
ideas, much more subtle than Stirner's, quickly appeared
in all branches of literature. Our polite letters are full of
"blonde beasts," and in social thought individualism again
raises its hand obstinately and with confidence of success.
Nietzsche has revived Stirner, and in him he contends with
a whole series of social theorems. First anarchy. Nietzsche's own philosophy is neither socialistic nor anarchistic. He knows only the strong, sovereign, self-contained individual. The masses, for whom social philosophy is usually concerned, are for Nietzsche the "much-too-many."
They are for the amusement and service of the "superior
man" (*Uebermensch*) - "beyond that let them go to the devil and statistics." His "superior men" are ends unto themselves, not for the "guidance" of the masses. He has no
place for an institutionalized aristocracy. Whoever has subdued man so as to become a "superior man" is an aristocrat, and he does not trouble himself about the worm be-
neath. No more does Nietzsche teach anarchism in the social sense. On the contrary, his "superior men," his "blonde
beasts," are the most rigorous despots. For them alone, the
select, there is no law, because they stand above the law.
For the masses "slave morals" must prevail. Stirner teaches
anarchism of an individualistic sort, not the communistic

anarchism so well known today. His theory is also more objective than Nietzsche's, not merely in its form of presentation, but also in its entire conception. In distinction from Nietzsche's individualism he fastens upon "egoism" as an objective psychical factor, and makes unlimited egoism an objective social postulate. Anarchism finds Stirner a support, but both he and Nietzsche give aid and comfort to the most recent movement in social philosophy, which is turning from social democracy to social aristocracy. The bent toward aristocracy is supposed to be toward satisfaction of individualistic wishes and inclinations.

Max Stirner / Sein Leben und Sein Werk by John Henry Mackay

Berlin: Schuster & Leeffler 1898

Book-length appreciation of Stirner.

The Eagle and the Serpent

No. 1 (February 15 1898)

Dedicated to the Philosophy of Life Enunciated by Niet
zsche, Emerson, Stirner, Thoreau and Goethe, THE EA
GLE AND THE SERPENT Labours for the Recognition
of New Ideals in Politics and Sociology, in Ethics and Phi
losophy, in Literature and Art.

The Eagle and the Serpent

No. 2 (April 15 1898)

Dedicated to the Philosophy of Life Enunciated by Niet
zsche, Emerson, Stirner, Thoreau and Goethe, THE EA
GLE AND THE SERPENT Labours for the Recognitio
of New Ideals in Politics and Sociology, in Ethics and Phi
losophy, in Literature and Art.

Course of Study for Beginners in Egoism: Will our friend
kindly assist us in making the following list as complete as
possible? We want references to English articles o
"Stirner" and on Egoism."

The men of future generations will yet win many a libert
of which we do not even feel the want. - Stirner.

The Eagle and the Serpent

No. 3 (June 15 1898)

Dedicated to the Philosophy of Life Enunciated by Nietzsche, Emerson, Stirner, Thoreau and Goethe, THE EA-
GLE AND THE SERPENT Labours for the Recognition
of New Ideals in Politics and Sociology, in Ethics and Philosophy, in Literature and Art.

Course of Study for Beginners in Egoism: Will our friends
kindly assist us in making the following list as complete as
possible?   We want references to English articles on
"Stirner" and on Egoism."

Sir: It seems to me an impossibility, or rather a curiosity to
edit a paper on the philosophy of Egoism and not to know
Max Stirner, the founder of the philosophy, at all, as you
seem to do. - John Henry Mackay. (With many others we
are anxiously awaiting the fulfillment of Herr Mackay's
dream - an English edition of Stirner. In the meantime
surely an egoist may follow himself without infringing on
Stirner's copyright. - ED.)

The Eagle and the Serpent

No. 4 (September 1 1898)

Dedicated to the Philosophy of Life Enunciated by Niet
zsche, Emerson, Stirner, Thoreau and Goethe, THE EA
GLE AND THE SERPENT Labours for the Recognition
of New Ideals in Politics and Sociology, in Ethics and Phi
losophy, in Literature and Art.

"Literary Acknowledgements." Uncredited.

Two works of great interest to egoists were published in
Berlin, March 15. We subjoin a description of these work
given by the author, John Henry Mackay, in *Liberty* c
New York for Dec., 1897. We hope to receive review
copies of them.

"After years of labour, I can to-day announce my biogra
phy of Max Stirner. It will bear the title: *Max Stirner: Sei
Leben und sein Werk*.

"Only years of labour and industry have enabled me to pe
in the place of the five lines (of which three were false
which constituted all that was then publicly known of th
life of the great thinker, a book of several hundred pages.

"In the first chapter I give an account of the early youth c
Stirner; in the second, of his years of study and teaching
All this without any other facts than mere dates to buil
on.

"The picture becomes more animated in the third chapte
where I treat of the circle of the 'Free' in Berlin, the onl
circle in which Stirner ever moved, and from which 'Ma
Stirner' (fourth chapter) speaks to us as a living personal
ty.

"The next chapter, the fifth, is devoted to a consideration c
his immortal work: *Der Einzige und sein Eigenthum*; an
the last treats of the last ten years of his life, when alread

he had been forgotten; and left to die in embarrassment and poverty ('The Last Decade').

"Simultaneously with my biography I publish a volume of Stirner's minor writings and his answer to his critics. It contains five essays and two rejoinders, - that is, everything that Stirner wrote except the great work of his life and his *Geschichte der Reaktion*.

"To-day Stirner is not so little known in Germany as he was eight years ago when I again discovered his work. In a cheap edition he is now in many hands; I wish he were in all hands. When will an English translation spread his influence in the New World?"

International Journal of Ethics

Vol. 9, No. 1 (October 1898), pp. 106-109

Book review of *Anarchism: A Criticism and History of the Anarchist Theory* by E. V. Zenker. Review by David G. Ritchie.

> The book before us is divided into three parts: Part I. Deal
> with early Anarchism, the Anarchist movements in the
> middle ages, etc., Proudhon, "Max Stirner" (Caspa
> Schmidt), etc. Part II. is entitled Modern Anarchism. On
> chapter is devoted mainly to Bakunin, another mainly t
> Kropotkin and Elisee Reclus, while a third gives a brief ac
> count of recent Anarchist writings in Germany, England
> and America. This chapter is confessedly incomplete so fa
> as America is concerned, as even a personal application t
> Mr. Tucker failed to procure a copy of his journal, *Liberty*
> Some account is given of Mr. Auberon Herbert's "Volun
> tary State;" but nothing is said of the sentimental anar
> chism of Mr. Edward Carpenter. Part III. treats of the Re
> lation of Anarchism to Science and Politics. [...] Th
> "Egoism" of Max Stirner, according to which property i
> "that over which I can assert my power" (a principle wide
> ly accepted in practice), is a theory at least as old as th
> Callicles and the Thrasymachus of Plato's *Dialogues*; an
> the philosophy of Proudhon, of Stirner and Bakunin, i
> spite of its use of Hegelian formula, is only a survival c
> the crude individualism of the Cynics and of the more au
> dacious Greek Sophists.

The Eagle and the Serpent

No. 5 (November 1 1898)

Dedicated to the Philosophy of Life Enunciated by Nietzsche, Emerson, Stirner, Thoreau and Goethe, THE EA-
GLE AND THE SERPENT Labours for the Recognition
of New Ideals in Politics and Sociology, in Ethics and Philosophy, in Literature and Art.

The Eagle and the Serpent

No. 6 (December 1 1898)

Dedicated to the Philosophy of Life Enunciated by Nietzsche, Emerson, Stirner, Thoreau and Goethe, THE EA-
GLE AND THE SERPENT Labours for the Recognition
of New Ideals in Politics and Sociology, in Ethics and Philosophy, in Literature and Art.

The Eagle and the Serpent

No. 7 (February 12 1899)

> Dedicated to the Philosophy of Life Enunciated by Niet
> zsche, Emerson, Stirner, Thoreau and Goethe, THE EA
> GLE AND THE SERPENT Labours for the Recognition
> of New Ideals in Politics and Sociology, in Ethics and Phi
> losophy, in Literature and Art.

"A War Against War Against War." Uncredited.

> A Common Denominator for Nietzsche and Stirner.
>
> Down with the Fool - the Battle Cry of all Free Spirits.
>
> I am the first-born of fabulously poor and idiotically honest
> parents. My mother, in the fatuous hope of producing an
> other prodigy as great as myself did not cease multiplying
> the race till the magic number seventeen was reached.
> Brought up in a family of so many of the unfit, I have been
> driven in a special degree to contemplate the problem of
> their rapid multiplication. The principal obstacle to
> progress is not the exploiter but the mass of ignorance and
> superstition upon which the exploiter relies to fight his bat
> tles. In their attitude towards the masses NIETZSCHE and
> STIRNER stand in inevitable alliance. Both of these over
> men fight the battle of the Free Spirits and if, ultimately
> they must fight each other, they will get to that combat the
> sooner if they close up their ranks and present a solid front
> to the unemancipated.
>
> What shall we do with the fools? That is the most impor
> tant question to-day both for Stirnerites and Nietzscheite
> Grant that we admit our duty is to educate these fools. Bu
> on that *dies irae* - on that great day of vengeance, when
> there is no time for further education; when in spite of al
> that education could do, the fools stand like La Vende
> before every entrenchment of error, driven by their infernal
> infatuation to the last ditch of death and devotion in de

fence of hoary wrongs - will we not on that day have to
sacrifice these infatuated fools as ruthlessly as we will their
lords and masters? On that day Stirner must declare war on
all slaves and fools. Nietzsche declares the war to-day.
And really, to a mind equally devoid of love and hate—
Proudhon's pure intellect—it must be evident that to have
any pity towards this God-soaked, Christ-soaked, servile
rabble, would be the greatest of crimes against progress.
Such an attitude were prudery. Their birth was an error, let
us pray it may be rectified. I heard a voice from heaven
saying, "Better still, go thou and rectify it." Perhaps a few
preliminary wars would make our task easier.

The fact that no one of our readers has renewed his sub-
scription to *E. AND S.* has convinced us that we are giving
the world more wisdom than it can assimilate. As this issue
is especially full of meat we have decided to give the world
till June 25 to digest it. No. 8 will appear on that day, the
deathday of STIRNER. We hope to make it a STIRNER
number, if this idea meets the approval of those at present
preparing an English edition of Stirner. The editor can keep
E. AND S. afloat as a quarterly with his present support.
Our friends can make it a monthly if they wish. Money
talks. Pledges of aid may be sent to E. McCall, 23, Linden
Mansions, Highgate Hill, London, N.

The American Journal of Semitic Languages and Literatures

Vol. 15, No. 3 (April 1899), pp. 17-48

"Theological and Semetic Literature / A Bibliographical Suppliment" by W. Muss-Arnolt.

> KRONENBERG, M. "Moderne Philosophen. Portrits und Charakteristiken." M.: Beck, '98 ; xi, 221 pp. M. 4.5o(?) Hermann Lotze - F. A. Lange - V. Cousin - L. Feuerbach M. Stirner.

The American Journal of Theology

Vol. 3, No. 2 (April 1899), pp. i-xxxii

"Theological and Semetic Literature / A Bibliographical Suppliment" by W. Muss-Arnolt.

> KRONENBERG, M. "Moderne Philosophen. Portrits und Charakteristiken." M.: Beck, '98 ; xi, 221 pp. M. 4.5o(?) Hermann Lotze - F. A. Lange - V. Cousin - L. Feuerbach M. Stirner.

The Monist

Vol. 9, No. 4 (July 1899), pp. 572-616

"Immorality as a Philosophic Principle" by Paul Carus.

The best known German expounders of Nietzsche's philosophy are Max Stirner, Rudolf Steiner, and Alexander Tille.
Professor Henri Lichtenberger of the University of Nancy
has become his interpreter in France, and Mr. Erwin Mc-
Call, the editor of *The Eagle and the Serpent*, in England
(See: M. Stirner, *Dier Einzige und seine Eigenschaft*. See
also R. Schellwein, *Max Stirner und Friedrich Nietzsche*).
A periodical *Der Eigene*, i. e., "he who is his own," announces itself as "a journal for all and nobody," and
"sounds the slogan of the egoists," by calling on them to
"preserve their ownhood." *Der Eigene* proposes to "antag-
onise all ideals of the brotherhood of man in the religious,
ethical, altruistic, social, and communistic fields." It de-
cries monopoly in every form, wages war against all
democratic programmes, all aspirations of equality, includ-
ing charity - manias in every form and slumming (*Pöbel-
beglückung*); it antagonises bureaucracy and all rules. It
does not expect social salvation from the socialistic aboli-
tion of private property, but from an unimpeded personal
appropriation, the realisation of which appears in a free
market and the unconditional *laissez faire*, *laissez passer*.
It expects to attain liberty by strengthening the single individual, which is to build up egoistical communities. It re-
pudiates the plan of revolutionising the masses, and the use
of violence. It stands up for the pathfinders in literature and
art, for personality, for that which is characteristic.

BLAKE

The Eagle and the Serpent

No. 9 (October 15 1899)

> Dedicated to the Philosophy of Life Enunciated by Niet
> zsche, Emerson, Stirner, Thoreau and Goethe, THE EA
> GLE AND THE SERPENT Labours for the Recognition o
> New Ideals in Politics and Sociology, in Ethics and Philos
> ophy, in Literature and Art.

Philosophie des Unbewussten by Ed- uard von Hartmann

Leipzig: Verlag von Wilhelm Friedrich 1900

> Höchst lehrreich ist in dieser Beziehung *Der Einzige un*
> *sein Eigenthum* von Max Stirner, ein Buch, das Niemane
> der sich für practische Philosophie interessirt, ungelese
> lassen sollte. Dasselbe unterwirft alle auf die Praxis Ein
> fluss habenden Ideen einer mörderischen Kritik, und weis
> sie als Idole nach, die nur soweit Macht über das Ic
> haben, als dieses ihnen eine solche in seiner sich selbs
> verkennenden Schwäche einräumt; es zermalmt in seine
> geistreichen und pikanten Weise mit schlagenden Gründe
> die idealen Bestrebungen des politischen, socialen und hu
> manen Liberalismus, und zeigt, wie auf den Trümmern a
> dieser in das Nichts ihrer Ohnmacht zusammengebroch
> enen Ideen nur das Ich der lachende Erbe sein kann. Wen
> diese Betrachtungen nur den Zweck hätten, die theoretis
> che Behauptung zu erhärten, dass Ich so wenig aus der
> Rahmen meiner Ichheit, als aus meiner Haut heraus kan
> so wäre denselben Nichts hinzuzufügen; indem aber Stirn
> er in der Idee des Ich den absoluten Standpunct für da
> Handeln gefunden haben will, verfällt er entweder demse
> ben Fehler, den er an den anderen Ideen, wie Ehre, Fre
> heit, Recht u. s. w. bekämpft hatte, und liefert sich au
> Gnade und Ungnade der Herrschsucht einer Idee au:

30

deren absolute Souveränität er anerkennt, aber nicht um der und jener Gründe willen anerkennt, sondern blind und instinctiv, oder aber er fasst das Ich nicht als Idee, sondern als Realität, und hat dann kein anderes Resultat, als die völlig leere und nichtssagende Tautologie, dass Ich nur meinen Willen wollen, nur meine Gedanken denken kann und dass nur meine Gedanken Motive meines Wollens werden können, eine Thatsache, die bei den von ihm bekämpften Gegnern ebenso unläugbar ist, als bei ihm. [...] Diese Einsicht, dass vom Standpuncte des Ich oder des Individuums aus die Willensverneinung oder Weltentsagung und Verzichtleistung aufs Leben das einzig vernünftige Verfahren ist, fehlt Stirner gänzlich, sie ist aber das sicherste Heilmittel gegen die Grossthuerei mit dem Standpuncte des Ich; wer die überwiegende Unlust, die jedes Individuum mit oder ohne Wissen im Leben erdulden muss, einmal verstanden hat, wird bald den Standpunct des sich selbsterhallen- und geniessen-wollendell; mit einem Worte des seine Existenz bejahenden Ich verachten und verschmähen; wer erst seinen Egoismus und sein Ich geringschätzt, wird auf dasselbe schwerlich noch als auf den absoluten Standpunct pochen, nach welchem alles sich zu richten habe, wird persönliche Opfer minder hoch anschlagen als sonst, wird minder widerwillig dem Resultate einer Untersuchung zustimmen, welche das Ich als eine blosse Erscheinung eines Wesens darstellt, das für alle Individuen ein und dasselbe ist.

The Philosophical Review

Vol. 9, No. 1 (January 1900), pp. 111-112

Book review of *Moderne Philosophen. Porträts und Charakteristiken* by M. Kronenberg (Munich: C. H. Beck 1899). Review by Grace Neal Dolson.

According to Dr. Kronenberg, the conflict between idealism and realism, which occupied the attention of the philosophic world between 1825 and 1865, is of especial importance, because there are indications that the present age of positivism will be followed by a return to idealism, and the same problems will again demand solution. The five philosophers chosen, Lotze, Friedrich Albert Lange, Cousin, Feuerbach, and Max Stirner, all belong to this period of conflict, and, taken together, exhibit its various aspects.

Revue Philosophique de la France et de l'Étranger

T. 49 (January to June 1900), pp. 335-336

"Livres Déposés Au Bureau De La Revue." Uncredited.

> Stirner (Max). *L'unique et sa propriété*, trad. Reclaire, in-8. Paris, Stock. […] Stirner (Max). *L'unique et sa propriété*, trad, de l'ail., in-8, Paris (éditions de la Revue Blanche).

Book review of *Studies from the Yale Psychological Laboratory (Travaux du laboratoire de Psychologie de Yale), vol. VI* by E. Scripture. Review by Fr. Paulhan.

> Max Stirner a combattu l'idéal, parce qu'il en a rencontré des théories qui lui ont et n'étaient sans doute sans Maisil n'a déplu, qui pas reproches. Pas vu clairement ce que c'était au fond que l'idéal et il n'a pas su analyser convenablement les donné es du problèm.

Revue de Métaphysique et de Morale

T. 8, No. 2 (March 1900), pp. 3-4

Book review of *L'Unique et sa Propriété* by Max Stirner (Paris: Revue blanche 1900). Review by Henri Lasvignes.

> A cet egard, Max Stirner est un precurseur. Son - posi
> tivisme glace - comme le nomme tres justement son tra
> ducteur, son egotisme transcendant renferment les diverse
> formules et font entrevoir les divers ideaux, assez pareil
> au fond, que nous proposent a tour de role l'atristogratiqu
> Nietzche.

The Eagle and the Serpent

No. 11 (July 1900)

"Our Memorial Issues." Uncredited.

> Beginning with our September Number, each issue of *E
> & S*. will have memorial quotations from the immortal fre
> spirits born in the month. We present herewith the name
> of which will be honored in this program [...] October: N
> etzsche, Stirner, Cervantes, Danton, Diderot, Bizet.

Revue Philosophique de la France et de l'Étranger

T. 50 (July to December 1900), pp. 314- 315

Book review of *Wille und Erkenntniss* by Robert Schellwien (Hamberg: A. Janssen 1899). Review by L. Arréat.

> M . Schellwien publie neuf Essais philosophique sous les titre suivants: I. La volontéet Max Stirner; II La volonté comme principe d'éducation; III. La volontéde connaître. IV. La volonté d'agir et l'éthique, V. Conclusions péda-gogiques; VI. La connaissance et la volonté dans Schopen-hauer; VIL La volonté humaine et Vidéede Dieu; VIII. La volonté dans la philosophie critique; IX. La volontéet la connaissance pour le senscommun.

Book review of *L'Unique et sa propriété* by Max Stirner with a preface by Henri Lasvignes (Paris: Editions de la Revue Blanche 1900). Review by Fr. Paulhan.

The Eagle and the Serpent

Vol. 2, No. 1 (September 1900)

"Our Memorial Issues." Uncredited.

> Beginning with our September Number, each issue of *E. & S.* will have memorial quotations from the immortal free spirits born in the month. We present herewith the names of which will be honored in this program [...] October: Ni-etzsche, Stirner, Cervantes, Danton, Diderot, Bizet.

The Eagle and the Serpent

Vol. 2, No. 2 (October 1900)

"John Henry Makay's Appreciation of Stirner." John
Mackay. Translated by Thomas Common.

|See complete essay after Bibliography.|

Annals of the American Academy of Political and Social Science

Vol. 16 (November 1900), pp. 166-176

"Index to Annals of the American Academy of Polit
ical and Social Science." Uncredited.

Stirner, 127

Revue de Métaphysique et de Morale

T. 8, No. 6 (November 1900)

"Livres nouveaux français." Uncredited.

Stirner

(M.) traduit par H. Lasvignes. - *L'Unique et sa propriété*,
vol. in-S de 471 p. *Revue Blanche*. - Mars, 3, II.

The Eagle and the Serpent

Vol. 2, No. 3 (January February March 1901)

"Kilkenny Column." Uncredited.

> Thomas Common on Stirner: My opinion Stirner is that he
> carries out false principles, such as are embodied in the
> American Declaration of Independence, to their logical
> conclusion - namely, the abolition all government. A most
> absurd conclusion certainly, but when people start with
> such falsehoods as "all men are created equal and are en-
> dowed with inalienable rights to life, liberty and the pur-
> suit of happiness," they are bound to reach absurd conclu-
> sions. "That all men are created equal." I hold this "truth"
> to be a self-evident absurdity. Black babies are always
> equal to white babies! Deformed babies are always equal
> to well-formed, healthy babies! And all babies are equal
> to the Siamese Twins when they were babies! (Our view
> *re* Stirner *contra* Nietzsche is given in Vol. 1. No. 7. Each
> is indispensable to the Free-Spirit, or to the Spirit strug-
> gling to be free. - Ed)

Historische Zeitschrift

Bd. 86, H. 2 (1901), pp. 273-276

"Allgemeine Deutsche Biographie" by K.

> Muster solcher Beschrankung auf das Wesentliche sind u.
> a. eine Anzahl Biographien, die O. Liebmann geliefert hat,
> namentlich die von Max Stirner.

Revue Philosophique de la France et de l'Étranger

T. 51 (January to June 1901), p. 224

"Livres Déposés Au Bureau De La Revue." Uncredited.

> Zoccoli, I gruppi anarchici degli Stati Uniti e l'opera d
> Max Stirner, i n-12. Modena, Vincezi.

The Eagle and the Serpent

Vol. 2, No. 4 (July 1901)

Uncredited.

> Special Stirner and Machiavelli Issues in preparation.

Revue de Métaphysique et de Morale

T. 9, No. 6 (November 1901), pp. 677-687

"Dans L'Enseignement de la Philosophie et de son Histoire" by Alfred Fouillée.

> De la 'immoralisme' de Nietzsche, qui revientaux théorie
> de l'Allemand Max Stirner du vieux Grec Calliclè
> sophistes et déclare au christianisme une guerre sans me
> ci.

Revue Philosophique de la France et de l'Étranger

T. 52 (July to December 1901), pp. 330- 331

Book review of *The Philosophy of Friedrich Nietzsche* by Grace Neal Dolson (New York: Macmillian Company 1901). Review by L. Arréat.

> Jusqu'ici, on avalt envisagé l'égoisme comme un simple fait; Nietzsche l'élève à la dignité d'un idéal; si incomplet que soit son systeme, c'est en cele plus que Max Stirner il a été novateur.

"Les Jugements De Nietzsche Sur Guyau: D'après Des Documents Inédits" by Alfred Fouillée.

> Pourquoi donc Zarathoustra se croit-il "unique," comme Max Stirner? Nous prétendonst ous tant que nous pouvons, nous autres moralistes, rectifierles jugements de l'humanité sur la meilleure conduite à suivre, et nous admettons tous qu'il y a des choses meilleuresque d'autre. [...] L'individu-alism effréné de Nietzsche demeure, comme celui de Max Stirner, en contradiction manifeste avec cette idée de soli-darité qui devient de plus en plus dominante aux yeux des biologistes et aux yeux des sociologues.

BLAKE

Revue Philosophique de la France et de l'Étranger

T. 53 (January to June 1902), pp. 98-102

Book review of *Essai sur l'individualisme (vol. in-12, 188p., de la Bibliothèque de philosophie contemporaine)* by E. Fournière. Review by G. Palante.

> Une foi sen possession de sa définition de l'individualisme
> M. F. critique de ce point de vue les diverses théories indi
> vidualistes (H. Spencer, Max Stirner, Tolstoï, Nietzsche).

Revue Philosophique de la France et de l'Étranger

T. 54 (July to December 1902), p. 651

Book review of *L'anarchia del punto de vista antropologico e sociale* by Perrone Capano (Naples: Edite par la Rassegna Italiana 1901). Review by Gaston Richard.

> Économiquement, il a fallu que le prolétariat pûtse constituer et engager la lutte contre le capital, sous la direction de chefs intellectuels qui ont modifié les doctrines révolutionnaires dans le sens de la lutte des classess, tels: Proudhon, Max Stirner, Bakounine, Kropotkine.

"Quelques Publications Récentes Sur La Morale" by J. Segond.

> Cette théorie morale n'entraîne pas du tout le panégoïsme, comme on le trouve formulé par Stirner, l'hédonisme ou l'eudémonisme; le fait de la d'une et part, l'impossibilité psychologiquede prendreson plaisir comme tel pour but, d'autre part, empêchent cette transformatiod ne la doctrine.

Book review of *Max Stirner et sa philosophie légoïsme* by V. Th. Savodnik. Review by Ossip-Lourié.

BLAKE

Revue Philosophique de la France et de l'Étranger

T. 55 (January to June 1903), pp. 601-633

"Esquisse D'une Philosophie Des Conventions Sociales" by Albert Schinz.

> Maisni Socratee, et Platon, ni le Christ et Bouddha, ni
> Comte et Spencer, ni Stirner et Nietzsche, ni Guyau e
> Fouillée n'ont donné une morale pour l'humanité, mai
> pour quelques personnes d'élite seulement, a cceptant leu
> doctrine spéciale delavie.

Journal of Political Economy

Vol. 11, No. 2 (March 1903), pp. 335-337

Book review of *Die vier Hauptrichtungen der so-
cialen Bewegung: Kritisch und vergleichend
dargestellt* by Benedict Friedlander (Berlin: S. Cal-
vary & Co., 1901). Review by Karl Detlev Jessen.

> Dr. Friedlander points to the indisputable fact that any de-
> cent, intelligent society, especially such a complex one as
> ours, must necessarily admit the authority of experts, not
> the least in the affairs of government. This necessity, how-
> ever much we may regret it, is nevertheless absolute, al-
> though totally ignored by the so-called communistic anar-
> chists, like Bakunin, Krapotkin, Tolstoi, Most. The indi-
> vidualistic forms of anarchistic theory, if the term "theory"
> be not a misapplication, the teaching of Max Stirner, John
> Henry Mackay, *et al.*, are, quite naturally, treated less *in
> extenso*. Perhaps it would have been appropriate to make
> some mention at least of the American Benjamin Tucker,
> whose doctrines are based on Prudhon's.

Revue Philosophique de la France et de l'Étranger

T. 56 (July to December 1903), pp. 93-103

Book review of *Nietzsche et l'immoralisme. Bibliothèque de philosophie contemporaine* by A. Fouillée (Paris: F. Alcan 1902). Review by G. Palante.

> Avant d'opposer Guyau à Nietzsche, M. Fouillée l'oppose
> Max Stirner, le précurseur de Nietzsche et le théoricienl
> plus outrancier ûe l'individualisme immoralist. [...] Le mc
> de Stirnerest vrai: "Un idéal n'est qu'un pion." [...] Ave
> K. Marx, Stirner, Nietzsche place les tâtonnements de l'ac
> tion avant les formules de la théorie.

The Monist

Vol. 14, No. 1 (October 1903)

"Contents of Volume XIV / Book Reviews an
Notes." Uncredited.

> Basch, Victor: *L'Individualisme Anarchiste / Max Stirne*
> 624

Giornale degli Economisti, Serie Seconda

Vol. 27 (No. 14) (November 1903), pp. 460-469

"Il Secondo Volume dei 'Systemes Socialists'" by Del Patero.

Questa religione antichissima e sempre nuova (va dalla leggenda dell'età dell'oro alla Resurre zione di Tolstoi) ha trovato nella grande industria moderna un terreno adattissimo al suo dolce seme (meno dolci saranno i frutti) e ha trovato in Marx il suo teologo sommo che ha piegato la scienza alla fede (1). Questa religione è seducente tanto che attira e conquista anche gran parte della borghesia, fiaccando così sempre più la resistenza dell 'élite che si sfascia (2). Certo i sentimenti umanitari sono utili, sono necessari anzi alla convivenza civile (3), e l'egoismo di Max Stirner e l'aristo crazia feroce di Nietzsche sono aberrazioni (4).

Revue Philosophique de la France et de l'Étranger

T. 57 (January to June 1904), pp. 684-685

"Livres Déposés Au Bureau De La Revue." Uncred ited.

> Basch. - *L'Individualisme anarchiste / Max Stirner*, In-8(Paris, F. Alean.

"Le Cynisme / Étude Psychologique" by Emile Tardieu.

> Max Stirner se fait professeur d'égoïsme; il exalte l'indivic ualisme absolu; chacun de nous est l'Uniqu. [...] Stirne s'attache à montrer la prépondérance invincible de l'é goïsme; impossible à chacun de sortirde soi: "Si j'ai d d'abord: J'aime le monde, je puis tout aussi bien ajouter présent: Je ne l'aime pas: car je l'anéantis comme j m'anéantis; j'en use et je l'use."

The Philosophical Review

Vol. 13, No. 3 (May 1904), pp. 390-392

"Notes." Uncredited.

RIVISTA DI FILOSOFIA E SCIENZE AFFINI, II, 5-6: E. Zamorani, "A chi legge;" R. Ardzig, "Sentire;" G. Vailati, "La teoria aristotelica della defi- nizione;" P. Orano, "Max Stirner in Italia;" F. Moingliano, "Un pubblicista, econo- mists, e filosofo del periodo Napoleonico (Melchiorre Gioia);" Rassegna di filosofia scientifica; Fra i libri; No- tizie; Indice degli articoli originali dell'annata 1903; Libri ricevute e sommari di riviste.

The American Journal of Psychology

Vol. 15, No. 3 (July 1904), pp. 458-462

Book review of *L'Individualisme Anarchiste / Max Stirner* by Victor Basch (Paris: Felix Alcan 1904). Review uncredited.

> Max Stirner was born in 1806 and died in 1856. He was in youth a pupil of Hegel and after taking his degree became teacher in a girls' high school in Berlin. Here, in 1844, he wrote his remarkable book entitled *Das Ich und sein Eigenthum*. In this he carried the affirmation of individualism and even selfishness to its utmost extreme as against Hegelism which subordinates persons to movements of the Zeit Geist. This book produced considerable sensation, but its advocacy of extreme and selfish egoism unsettled the author. He had to resign his position and thenceforth lived in squalor doing hack work. His second wife, also an extreme socialist and from whom he was divorced and who lived on till 1896 in London, is said to have sunk very low. Stirner would have been almost forgotten had it not been for the interest in Nietzsche of whom he is called one of the precursors. This prompted John Henry MacKay to write Stirner's life and it also prompted this book.

Book review of *Moderne Philosophen* by M. Kronenberg (Munchen: C. H. Beck 1899). Review uncredited.

> These five essays, with the exception of that on Ludwig Feuerbach, have appeared previously. One chapter each is given to Hermann Lotze, Fr. Alb. Lange, Victor Cousin, Ludwig Feuerbach, and Max Stirner.

The Monist

Vol. 14, No. 4 (July 1904), pp. 623-624

Book review of *L'Individualisme Anarchiste / Max Stirner* by Victor Basch (Paris: Felix Alean Editeur 1904). Review uncredited.

> Max Stirner is a modern thinker who is closely allied to Nietzsche, yet he is more systematic than the inventor of the overman. He bases all his views upon the valuation of the individual and thus stands for the uniqueness of each personality. His system of thought may be briefly charac- terised, as is done by Professor Basch, as anarchistic indi- vidualism, but it is under stood that Stirner is not an anar- chist of violent temper. He does not see in anarchism a mere destruction of the present form of society but a new organization in which the individual feels its uniqueness, by being freed of all religious chains, of all gods, of moral- ity, of all conventions in which it can manifest all its ener- gies and level all its powers, be his own creator and own proprietor, look with contempt upon every outside influ- ence and to be unhampered by any scruple or regard. Pro- fessor Basch characterises Stirner "the unique one." He describes the background from which his theories proceed and investigates the peculiarity of this apostle of anarchist- sic individualism with appreciation of his ingenious work.

The Philosophical Review

Vol. 13, No. 4 (July 1904), pp. 488-489

"Notices of New Books" by I. M. Bentley.

> *L'individualisme Anarchiste / Max Stirner.* Par Victor
> Basch. Paris F. Alcan, 1904. - PP. vi, 294. 6 fr. [...] *Riv-*
> *ista Di Filosofia E Scienze Affini*, II, 5-6: P. Orano, Max
> Stirner in Italia.

Revue de Métaphysique et de Morale

T. 12, No. 5 (September 1904), p. 5

Book review of *L'Individualisme Anarchiste / Max
Stirner* by Victor Basch (Paris: Biblioteque generale
des Sciences sociales 1904). Book review uncredited.

> Le livre de M. Basch est un de ces rares ouvrages dont on
> peut dire qu'ils epuisent presque leur sujet. Il decr
> d'abord le - milieu d'idees - ou s'est forme Stirner - suit le
> premieres essais du philosophe - analyse, puis examin
> methodiquement son oeuvre capitale: *L'Unique et s*
> *Propiete*.

Modern Philology

Vol. 2, No. 2 (October 1904), pp. 151-172

"Die Audienz beim Fürsten / Geschichte Eines Literarischen Motivs" by Richard M. Meyer.

> Da soll Helmholtz dem Robert Mayer oder Joule, Nietzsche gar dem Max Stirner die Grundgedanken entnommen haben; Lessing und Leibniz werden als Hehler angeklagt, deren Schriften ein ganzes Lager angeeigneter Gedanken darstellen, und andererseits sollen Giordano Bruno, ja Gottscheddie eigentlichen Thater der geistigen Thaten ganzer Jahrhunderte sein, von denen sie stillschweigend ausgebeutet worden waren!

Revue de Métaphysique et de Morale

T. 12, No. 6 (November 1904)

"Livres français nouveau and Theses de Docorat" Uncredited.

> Livres français nouveau: Basch (V.). - *L'individualisme anarchiste* / *Max Stirner*,1 vol. in-8, vi-29i p., Alcan. - Septembre, 5, 11 [...] Le Dantec (F.). - "Stirner et Nietszche," 1 vol. in-8 de 116 p. *Societe nouvelle d'edition et de librairie*. - Septembre, 6, 1. [...] Theses de Docorat: Lévy (A). - I. "Stirner et Nietzsche.- II. La philosophiede Feuerbach." - Mai, 23, I.

BLAKE

Revue Philosophique de la France et de l'Étranger, Troisième Table Générale Des Matières: Contenues Dans Les Années 1896 A 1905

(1905), pp. 1-46

"Table Analytique Des Matières" by J. Clavière.

> Cantella: *Giacomo Leopardi et Max Stirner*, 1905, I, 33
> [...] Savodnik: "Max Stirner et sa philosophie de l'ego
> isme," 1902, II, 541 [...] Basch: *L'individualisme anar
> chiste / Max Stirner*, 1903, II, 656.

Revue Philosophique de la France et de l'Étranger

T. 59 (January to June 1905), pp. 332-335

"Rivista Filosofica, 1904" by J. Segond.

> F. Cantella. - *Giacomo et Max Stirner*. Leopardi et Stirne
> subissent des influence asnalogues, arrivent au même n
> hilisme. Mais Stirner est purement négateur, tandis qu
> Leopardi reconnaîtle rôle social de l'illusion, et assigne
> l'imagination le premie rôle dans la vie.

"Le Mouvement Philosophique En Russie / Les Slavophiles" by F. Lannes.

> La condamnation définitive d'une semblable tendance s
> trouve dans un livre "absurde par la forme, ignoble par l
> caractère moral, mais d'une logique absolue: *Der Einzelr
> und sein Eigenthum* de Max Stirner."

The Philosophical Review

Vol. 14, No. 2 (March 1905), pp. 260-264

"Notes." Uncredited.

> *Rivista Filosofica*, VII, 5: [..] F. Cantella, *Giacome Leop-ardi et Max Stirner*.

Mind, New Series

Vol. 14, No. 54 (April 1905), pp. 284-291

"Philosophical Periodicals" by J. L. M'Intyre.

> *Rivista Filosofica*. Annovi., vol.vii., Fasc. v., Novem-ber-December, 1904. […] F. Cantella *Giacomo Leopardi e Max Stirner*. […] Leopardi was not only the great poet of the nineteenth century, but is destined to be the great philosopher of the twentieth century. Anticipating all Max Stirner's ideas, he has provided a remedy for them by pointing out the beneficent part played by illusion in life.

Revue Philosophique de la France et de l'Étranger

T. 60 (July to December 1905)

"Analyseset Comptes Rendus." Uncredited.

> Basch. - *L'individualisme anarchiste / Max Stirner* 656

Max Stirners Lehre / Mit einem Auszug aus "Der Einzige und sein Eigentum" by A. Martin

Leipzig: Otto Wigand 1906

> Ich fand es nur in der Ordnung, das Stirnersche Buch *De*
> *Einzige und sein Eigentum* in der hiesigen Universität-bib
> liothet (in Berlenen) in die philosophische Abteilung de
> lästern - wo ich es jüngst entdedte - gestellt ist. Stirner is
> Philosoph, whofür ich ihn schon lange hielt.

Stirner / Grundlagen zun Verstädnis des Werkes "Der Einzige und sein Eigentum" by Herman Schultheiss

Ratibor: Gerdruckt bei F. Lindner 1906

> Eine wissenschaftliche Behandlung der Gedanken Stirne
> wird sich nicht lediglich an das historische Interesse wer
> den, sondern vielleicht noch lebhaster das systematische i
> Anspruch nehmen. Denn Starrens Buch, *Der Einzige un*
> *sein Eigentum* tann ohne eine forgfälitte Grötrennung de
> Egoismusgedanten gar nicht verstanden werden, und wen
> das, was seit sechzig Jahren für und gegen Stirne
> geschrieben worden ist, Geschwäs ist, so liegt es zur
> grössten Teil daran, dass diese Erörettung fehlt.

PMLA, Vol. 21, Appendix. Proceedings of the Twenty-Fourth Annual Meeting of the Modern Language Association of America, 1906

(1906), pp. lii-xixday

Fifth session, Saturday, December 29: A presentation on "The Superman" by Professor Thomas Stockham Baker of the Jacob Tome Institute.

> The word and its history. - A new phase of transcendentalism. - Recent interest in the subject; the theories of Max Stirner; Guyau and his significance; Nietzsche and the Superman; the cult of the Superman in Germany; the increasing importance of Nietzsche for literature; Nietzsche's influence outside of Germany; English borrowings from his philosophy. - The permanent and ephemeral elements in his teachings. - Twenty-five minutes.

Revue Philosophique de la France et de l'Étranger

T. 63 (January to June 1907), pp. 337-365

"Anarchisme Et Individualisme / Étude De Psychologie Sociale" by G. Palante.

Les mots anarchisme et individualisme sont fréquemmen employés comme synonymes. Des penseurs, fort différen ds'ailleurs les uns des autres, sont qualifiés un peu a hasard tantôt d'anarchistes, tantôt d'individualistes. C'es ainsi que Ton parle indifféremment de l'anarchismeou d l'individualisme stirnerien, de l'anarchisme ou de l'individ ualisme nietzschéen, de Panarchisme ou de l'individual isme barrésien, etc. Dans d'autres cas pourtant, cette identi fication des deux termes n'est pas regardée comme poss ble. On dit couramment: l'anarchisme proudhonien, l'ana chisme marxiste, l'anarchisme syndicaliste; mais on ne di pas: l'individualisme proudhonien, marxiste, syndicaliste On parlera bien d'un anarchisme chrétienou tolstoïen; ma non d'un individualisme chrétienou tolstoïen.

Mind, New Series

Vol. 16, No. 62 (April 1907), pp. 281-298

Book review of *Schopenhauer und Nietzsche Ein Vortgraszyklus* by Georg Simmel (Leipzig: Duncker & Humblot 1907). Review by David Morrison.

> Prof. Simmel quite rightly protests against regarding Nietzsche as a modern representative of the Sophists, or a new edition of Max Stirner. His concentration of value in the individual receives objective significance as a stage in the development of humanity. He made Personalism into an objective ideal, and thereby separated it completely from Egoism properly so-called: *Der Egoismus will etwas haben, der Personaltsrnius will etwas sein*.

The Philosophical Review

Vol. 16, No. 3 (May 1907), pp. 237-265

"Contemporary Philosophy in Germany" by Oscar Ewald. Mentions *Schopenhauer und Nietzsche* by Georg Simmel (Leipzig: Duncker and Hubolt 1906).

> Simmel insists that the creator of *Zarathustra* should not be confused with the moral subjectivists, the anarchistic sceptics, nor with Max Stirner and the Sophists.

The North American Review

Vol. 185, No. 616 (June 7 1907), pp. 332-337

Book review of *The Ego and His Own* by Max Stirner (translation by Steven T. Byington. New York: Benjamin R. Tucker 1907). Review by James Huneker.

[See complete essay after Bibliography.]

Franz Overbeck und Friedrich Nietzsche / eine Freundschaft by Carl Albrecht Bernoulli.

Jena: Eugen Diederichs 1908

"Ich," sagte [Nietzsche], "da habe ich mich in Klinger schön getäuscht. Das war ein Philister, nein mit dem Fühle ich mich nicht verwandt; aber Stirner, ja der!" Dabei ging ein feierlicher Zug über sein Gesicht. Während ich mit Spannung in seine Züge blickte, veränderten sich diese wieder, er machte etwas wie eine scheuchende, abwehrende Bewegung mit der Hand und sagte flüsternd: "Nun habe ich es Ihnen doch gesagt, und ich wollte nicht davon sprechen. Vergessen Sie es wieder. Man wird von einem Plagiat reden, aber Sie werden das nicht tun, das weiss ich." [Translation by Trevor Blake: "I was wrong about the beauty of Klinger. He was a philistine. But Stirner - yes!" Having said this, a solemn expression came over Nietzsche's face. He made a dismissive gesture with his hand and whispered, "Now I've told you what I did not want to tell you. Forget it. They will talk about my plagiarism of Stirner, but I know you will not do that."]

International Journal of Ethics

Vol. 18, No. 4 (July 1908), pp. 526-530

"Books Received" by J. S. Mackenzie.

The Ego And His Own. By Max Stirner. Translated from the German by Steven T. Byington. With an introduction by J. L. Walker. New York: Benj. R. Tucker, 1907. PP. xx, 506.

The Philosophical Review

Vol. 17, No. 4 (July 1908), pp. 400-426

"German Philosophy in 1907" by Oscar Ewald.

Although the idea of the suprahuman is common to Niet
zsche, Kant, and Wagner, the point that distinguishes Niet
zsche from the latter two is the fact that he does not look
for the overman in the sphere of universality, in the reli
gious or aesthetic universe, but rather in the sphere of indi
viduation. It was this intensive nuance of individualism
that appeared to point from Nietzsche to Max Stirner, the
author of the remarkable work *Der Einzige und sei*
Eigentum. Stirner's influence in modern Germany has as
sumed astonishing proportions, and moves in general par
allel with that of Nietzsche. The two thinkers are regarde
as exponents of essentially the same philosophy. This view
is approximated by Max Messer in his monograph *Ma*
Stirner [*Die Litteratur*, ed. by Georg Brandes, Verlag Bar
und Marquardt, Berlin] who sees Stirner's greatness in th
fact that he was the first to show the illusory character c
impersonal ideals and to recognize nothing as value tha
cannot justify its title to personal value. Messer is right i
his contention that true idealism cannot suffer by this bu
on the contrary is fostered. He refers the apparently in
moralistic character of Stirner to his attempt to set up a
iron opposition to the abstract moral dogma of the past. I
general he regards Stirner's work as an immense advanc
over Hegel's attempt to convert individual reality into
fabric of abstractions. Little as one may contest the impor
tance of Stirner, who was an energetic rather than pro
found thinker, still one has good cause to be cautious i
comparing him with Nietzsche. Individualism is Stirner
last word, but not Nietzsche's. [...] On the other hand, Ern
Horneffer is decidedly wrong when he fancies in his work
Wege zum Leben, [Klinkhardt, Leipzig 1907] that he is
follower of Nietzsche. For his values are extreme, indivic
ualistic values, approximating the philosophy of Stirne
The aim of human life is not surrender to a universal, as t

God or the universe, but unceasing shaping, separation, and individuation.

Annals of the American Academy of Political and Social Science

Vol. 32, Tariff Revision (September 1908), pp. 176-189

Book review of *Anarchism* by Paul Eitzbacher (1908). Book review uncredited.

> Johann Kaspar Schmidt, commonly known as Max Stirner, founded his teaching on the supreme law of personal welfare. If each man looks to his own welfare, law is unnecessary, because in order to attain the highest personal welfare it is often necessary for man to transgress the law.

Mind, New Series

Vol. 18, No. 71 (July 1909), pp. 443-446

Book review of *Philosophische Stromungen der Gegenwart* by Ludwig Stein (Stuttgart: Enke 1908). Review by Herbert W. Blunt.

> Individualism is of course represented in the main by Nietzsche, but Max Stirner also finds a place.

BLAKE

The Philosophical Review

Vol. 18, No. 5 (September 1909), pp. 514-535

"German Philosophy in 1908" by Oscar Ewald.

> Last year, writings occasioned by Darwin's centennial of
> fered proof, even in this field, of the growth of idealism
> Biological naturalism has lost ground both in epistemolo
> gy and ethics. This comes clearly to view in Max Stirner'
> work, *Die Leire Darwins in ihren letzten Folgen* (Berlin
> Hofmann and Co., pp. vi, 244) a second edition of whic
> was quickly called for. The work is to be recommended t
> the attention of everyone interested in philosophical an
> moral problems, especially to persons vacillating betwee
> naturalism and idealism. It offers a rigid demonstratio
> that a genuinely human ethics cannot be based on the pos
> tulates of the theory of selection, and that the principle o
> the struggle for existence can establish only the bru
> morality of might. Stirner shows with logical care tha
> wherever ethical ideas are developed from naturalistic pos
> tulates, contradictions and arbitrariness are involved. An
> so one may regard this book as an indirect support of ide
> alism.

Ten Blind Leaders of the Blind by Arthur M. Lewis

Chicago: Charles H. Kerr 1910

Now, let us trace the development of Stirner's Egoism. Stirner accepts Feuerbach's explanation of the imaginary origin of the theological idea. But he complains that - as Feuerbach only abolishes one abstraction Deity to set up in its place another abstraction - humanity - we are really no better off than we were before. We are rescued from the tyranny of one abstraction to be under the obedient slavery of another. [...] Stirner contends that this, instead of abolishing the slavery of the individual, only gives him a new master. Although this new master is conceived as being inside the individual, it is no more the individual than the master who was outside: "It is all one in the main whether I think of the essence as in me or outside me." In addition to this abstraction Humanity, the individual is to be enslaved by a host of others; justice, freedom, the fatherland, the good, the true, and the beautiful. All these have great causes which must be served. The only cause which a man must not serve is his own cause. But, demands Stirner, do these tyrants practice any of the self-abnegation they require from us? Not in the least; they serve only themselves. [...] "Nothing is more to me than myself." This leads Stirner to preach "self-ownership." The individual should free himself from the domination of all things outside himself and serve himself alone. And now we see how completely Stirner has severed himself from the world of real things the world as it actually is. How would this self-owned, self-centered, self-dependent individual dress? Not in cloth, surely. The man who dresses in cloth does so because he is being "served" by thousands who toil in the textile industry, and instead of independently severing himself, interdependently serves them in return or he is a social Parasite. [Egoism] could have no application or force in a class society.

The Duty of Altruism by Ray Madding McConnell

New York: The Macmillan Company 1910

> When the altruist says that the mother is not moved to the
> nursing and care of her infant through any calculation o<
> her own pleasure and profit, the egoist replies that the sym
> pathetic feeling on the part of the mother is her own feel
> ing, and that she is moved by this feeling and consequentl<
> by a self-regarding motive And when Max Stirner, th<
> arch-egoist, says "She can will only her own volitions
> think only her own thoughts, feel only her own feelings
> and only her own thoughts and feelings can be the motive
> of her will," it is replied from the other side, "Of cours<
> she alone can be the *subject* of her thought, feeling an<
> will; but it is an altogether different question as to whethe<
> she alone can be the *object* of her thought, feeling an<
> will." [...] Max Stirner said that a man could no more ge<
> outside of seeking his own interests in action than he coul<
> get outside of his own skin.

The Economic Bulletin

Vol. 3, No. 3 (September 1910), pp. 309-385

"Recent Publications." Uncredited.

> Smith (Adam) *Der Reichtum der Nationen* (According ■
> the translation by Max Stirner and the English edition b■
> Cannan (1904), published by H. Schmidt, 2 vols. Leipzi<
> A Kröner, '10. Pp. vi, 245; iv, 324. 1 m ea.

Dora Marsden

The Famous Sayings of Max Stirner

Chicago: Thurland & Thurland. Circa 1911 - 1916.

Book-length quotes from *The Ego and Its Own*, with editorial by Ragnar Redbeard (author of *Might is Right*).

> Intellectual forerunner of Nietzsche. "The Sayings of Stirner." Reprinted from *Redbeard's Review* (Lond). A condensed summary of Stirner's root and branch philosophy. Gives all of Stirner's best arguments for popular instruction and reference in a nutshell. Translated from *Der Einige*. [...]
>
> Max Stirner's great work *The Ego and His Own* is at last accessible to English readers. More than half a century ago this book was born. A conspiracy of silence and fear killed it for a period. The lords of the book world strangled it. Scarcely any knowledge of its far reaching concepts ever reached outside of a small ring of scholars. To them it was an inexhaustible gold mine of magnificent affirmation and bold deduction.
>
> Because of his thoroughgoing style of argument we earnestly recommend Stirner to all students of sociology or religion, who are of an intrepid and penetrative mind and who honestly and sincerely wish to go sheer down to the very roots of things. Assuredly he will take them there and plainly show them how blank brazen deceits have been evolved into "admitted certainties" and "sacred truths of God."
>
> Unlike the merely rationalistic school, however, Stirner has something substantial to propound - something that arouses the material hopes of all strong and venturesome characters. Like *Might is Right* this truly great work abounds in epigram and bristles with aggressiveness. Every sentence and paragraph is alive with stupendous inferences. Hence if you are a thinking man of any kind or calibre

ibre you must not neglect the grim old Stirner, who reasons everything out in such a truly awful fashion.

Send for a copy. Read it slowly. Consider the bearing of every chapter upon the satanic environment in which most men grind out their lives for less than nothing. Translate the iron logic of this root-and-branch philosopher into tears of your own psychology and experience. The chances are that Stirner will find out all your pet fallacies and tumble all your "dead sure things" about your ears. It is safe to say that he knows more than you ever did. Hence he is the right man to become acquainted with. What's the use of soaking your mind in authors who only echo and re-echo your own hallucinations? How can you ever learn anything that way?

In |some| places the book is a terror to read, but when you do read it, you have mastered something that you will never be able to forget as long as you live. Cloth bound. Well printed. 500 pages. Price $1.00

Vierteljahrschrift für Sozial- und Wirtschaftsgeschichte

9. Bd., H. 4 (1911), p. 604

Book review of *L'Individualisme économique et so-cial, ses origines, son évolution, ses formes con-temporaines* by Albert Schatz (Paris 1907). Review by J. Letaconnoux.

> Au XIX siecle, il suit l'evolution de la doctrine classique
> qui se complete avec Dunoyer et J. St. Mill; il decrit le lib-
> eralisme orthodoxe de Bastiat, le liberalisme politique d
> Taine et de de Tocqueville, le liberalisme chretien de L
> Play a Marc Sangnier, et enfin l'individualisme sous toute
> ses formes, sociologique avec Herbert Spencer, arnachis
> avec Proudhon et Max Stirner...

American Journal of Sociology

Vol. 16, No. 5 (March 1911), pp. 712-720

"Recent Literature." Uncredited.

> Smith (Adam) *Der Reichtum der Nationen*. Nach der U
> bers. von Max Stirner u. d. engl. Ausg. von Cannon (190
> hrsg. von H. Schmidt (Jena). 2 Bd. 8vo. Leipzig: Kröne
> '10. Pp. vi, iv + 245, 324.

The Monist

Vol. 21, No. 3 (July 1911), pp. 376-397

"Max Stirner, The Predecessor of Nietzsche" by Paul Carus.

> [See complete essay after Bibliography.]

The Philosophical Review

Vol. 20, No. 5 (September 1911), pp. 586-588

"Notes" by E. G. Spaulding.

> We give below a list of the articles, etc., in the current philosophical periodicals [...] *The Monist*, XXI, 3: Editor, "Max Stirner, the Predecessor of Nietzsche."

Revue Philosophique de la France et de l'Étranger, Quatrième Table Générale Des Matières: Contenues Dans Les Années 1906 A 1912

(1912), pp. 35-122

"Table Analytique Des Matières" by J. Clavière.

> Personnalité: L'idée de la personnalité chez Max Stirner (Iline), 1912, I, 671. [...] Stirner: Deux types d'immoralisme (G. Palante), 1908, I, 274.

The Freewoman

Vol. 1, No. 8 (January 11 1912), pg. 148 - 149

"Millenium" by Selwyn Weston.

> There is no influence so fraught with disaster to the
> modern mind as intellectual snobbery, for the as-
> sumption of knowledge is an ample barrier against
> new ideas, clamouring for admission to the intelli-
> gence. Nietzsche's elaboration of Max Stirner's Su-
> perman has his place in the scheme of things, but he
> is not *final*. He is not an end, but a means; and the
> end is a unity against which he, enduring, will war.

Revue Philosophique de la France et de l'Étranger

T. 73 (January to June 1912), pp. 670-671

"Voprossi filossofii i psychologuii. Janvier-décembre 1911" by Ossip-Lourié.

G. Scherchenievitch. La justificationdu droit. L'auteur parle d e Proudhon, de Bakounine, de Max Stirner, de Kropotkine, de Tolstoï, etc. et conclut que la contraint est la base de l'État et du droit. Tant que nos propres intérêtsne sont pas en jeu, cette contraintenous semble odieuse; cependant, il faut reconnaîtreque "l'autorité et le droit sont indispensables à la viesociale." [...] J. A. Iline. *L'idée de la personnalité chez Max Stirner.* Stirner connaissait très bien les idéalistes allemands, notamment Fichteet Hegel; on ne peuten douter après une analyse attentivede son livre *Der Einzige und sein Eigentum* (*L'Unique et sa propriété*). Il est impossible de trouver chez Stirner une théorie plus ou moins systematique personnalité. Les termes mêmes, L'individu, la personalite ne sont jamais empoyes par lui. Il aime le terme "*Ich*" et aussi "*Ich, der Mensch.*" Pour lui, le moi, c'est "l'hommeréel," *der wirkliche Mensch.* L'idée constructive n'est pas absente, elle est seulement moins bien présentée dans l'œuvre de Stirner que l'idée destructive. Stirner ne doit pas être considéré comme un amoraliste. Son amoralisme est un simple "écartde sa doctrine," on ne peut pas l'envisager comme la base même de sa philosophie.

BLAKE

The Freewoman

Vol. 2, No. 38 (August 8 1912), p. 221 - 222

"The Growing Ego" by Dora Marsden.

> We have just laid aside one of the profoundest of human documents, Max Stirner's *The Ego and his Own*. A correspondent has asked us to examine Stirner's doctrine, and shortly we intend to do so. Just now we are more concerned to overcome its penetrative influence on our own minds, by pointing out the abrupt and impossible termination of its thesis rather than to point out its profound truth. Sapient, grey-clad truths follow close-pressed one upon the heels of another, wearing the sincerity of unstudied reflection. It reads almost like an old man muttering. From point to point Stirner moves on, deposing all things and all powers in order that he may enthrone the Ego. The entire conceptual world, the complete thought-realm he attacks and overcomes and lays at the feed of the Ego. Morality, religion, God, and man are all brought low. They no longer rule as external powers influencing the Ego. To the Ego they are as his footstool. Scarcely so, indeed, for save as error, they do not exist. The Ego is supreme, and reigns in his lonely kingdom. His joy lies in self-enjoyment, he reigns over himself; his business is "to use himself up." It seems a strange anti-climax, at first sight - so great means, and such small ends. The solution, we must believe, is to be found in the unfolding of the content of the term - the "Satisfaction of the Ego." If the Ego is supreme, its satisfaction is necessary. What it seeks after must find; what it wants it must have. If its satisfaction do not already exist, they must be created. Hence, if the Ego needs the realisation in itself or morality, or religion or God, then, by virtue of its own supremacy, the realisation will be forthcoming.

The New Freewoman

Volume 1 Number 6 (September 1 1913), pg. 104 - 106

"Views and Comments" by Dora Marsden.

> "We are freeborn men, and wherever we look we see our-
> selves made servants of egoists. Are we therefore to be-
> come egoists too? Heaven forbid! We want rather to make
> egoists impossible. We want to make them all 'raga-
> muffins'; all of us must have nothing, that 'all may have.'
> So say the Socialists." Thus Stirner, more than half a cen-
> tury ago, in the most powerful work that has ever emerged
> from a single human mind. The quotation comes very pat
> to-day, when "ragamuffin" has become - as Stirner prophe-
> sied it would - a term of respect. The ragamuffin is the per-
> son who is devoid of property and also who has no objec-
> tions to so being. He is the ideal citizen, the pattern in
> whose presence the defective property-owning ones feel
> themselves rightly under reproach. The nobler among
> these latter are merely hesitating in their choice of the best
> means of divesting themselves of their property that they
> may become ragamuffins too, when they will have become
> good citizens, no longer a menace to the equal authority of
> the State. This is not irony: it is the description of an actual
> process. Slowly, all persons are consenting to be divested
> of their real property: the noble, by request; the less noble,
> by "arrangement." Real property, land, the State can easily
> obtain by arrangement, i.e. by buying it at the modest mar-
> ket price (oh, shades of Norman William) of good
> linoleum. The method by which the State may acquire too,
> the token of property, money, has not as yet been precisely
> fixed up, but doubtless will be so quite satisfactorily in due
> order of time.

The New Freewoman

Vol. 1, No. 7 (September 15 1913), pg. 123 - 126

"Views and Comments" by Dora Marsden.

> With this present issue of *The New Freewoman*, the distin
> guished American scholar who has done English-speakin
> peoples a service of inestimable value by his translation o
> Max Stirner's work into English as *The Ego and His Ow*
> Mr. Steven T. Byington, opens a series of articles on "In
> terference with Environment," a series which we take to b
> concerned with the limitations of the liberty of the indivic
> ual in the social community. We shall be among the mos
> interested of Mr. Byington's readers and possibly amon
> his critics. Be that as it may, we can prophesy in advanc
> that our criticism will not be that liberty is laid in fetter
> Our only concern is with the means and necessity for sel
> defence.

The New Freewoman

Vol. 1, No. 8 (October 1 1913), pg. 156 - 157

"Lego et Penso" by Benjamin R. Tucker.

> |Quoting *Idee Generale de la Revolution au Dixneuviem
> Siecle* by Pierre-Joseph Proudhon| "The law is clear, th
> sanction still more so. Three articles, which make but one
> that is the whole social contract. Instead of making oath
> God and his prince, the citizen swears upon his conscienc
> before his brothers, and before Humanity. Between thes
> two oaths there is the same difference as between slaver
> and liberty, faith and science, courts and justice, usury ar
> labour, government and economy, non-existence and b
> ing, God and man."

Leaving out the words "good," "wicked," "brute," and "Humanity," which are mere surplusage here, this extract, I think, would have been acceptable even to Max Stirner as a charter for his "Union of the Free," an appreciation of the importance of which is necessary to a complete appreciation of Stirner's political philosophy. If Miss Marsden knows of any idea originating in America, or developed there, of greater moment or larger dimensions than that presented in this page from France, she will do me a very great service in pointing it out.

The New Freewoman

Vol. 1, No. 10 (November 1 1913), pg. 185 - 196

"What is 'Sanity'" by Alice Groff.

There are men with minds of a low order of intelligence, because of ignorance of the higher scientific facts of life - minds of what is called the "common sense" type that have not had the education and wide contact that gives broad knowledge - which are nevertheless perfectly sane minds, minds which reason freely within the range of the facts which they possess - minds that are always plastic to the admission of a new fact that may come within their ken. There are also people of almost cosmic intelligence, who are utterly unable to reason because of "feeling-bias" or prejudice - utterly unable to co-ordinate fully into any reasoning process the enormous number of facts they may have knowledge of - minds that are insane to the degree and intensity of this inability. Max Stirner's was a mind that might be called cosmically insane; his "feeling-bias" or prejudice in favour of the importance of his own ego, inhibiting any co-ordination whatever of all of the other facts of life.

The New Freewoman

Vol. 1, No. 11 (November 15 1913), pg. 203 - 205
and page 219

"Views and Comments" by Dora Marsden.

We frankly do not understand why Mr. Tucker, an egoist
and Stirner's English publisher, does not see the necessity
of clearing current language of padding as a preliminary o
egoistic investigation. It is a task which pioneers in a new
branch of science are always faced with. Stirner himsel
worked like a navvy at the job. As for Proudhan, we ar
entirely beyond the reach of the verdicts of opinion amon
"those who know," and are not moved by the fact tha
Proudhan was at the "zenith of his power" when he wrot
"*L'dee generale de la revolution au XIXe siecle*."

It should please Mr. Tucker, who has published most c
Proudhan's works, to know that we *have* at least read tha
work from which he extracted the quotation in question
and that its quality appears to us to be exactly on a leve
with the workings of a private telephone, lucid and clea
for respectable intervals, then a buzz which churns in
one's head for quite long spells until one is tempted to pu
up the receiver - or close the book. Then it breaks out agai
astonishingly clear. When he is looking at things as the
exist he is a strong searchlight; when he is trying to wo
his readers to his solutions, he uses methods of cajoler
which are positively repellant, and make style a thing n
to be mentioned. Consider for instance the entire prefac
"A la bourgeosie": Mr. Lloyd George addressing a Bapti
Conference would be capable of it: or Mr. Will Crool
working on the emotions of a gathering of the I.L.P. Con
pare Stirner on the same subject! Yet writing exactly i
the middle of the last century when the theory of represen
tative government was midway in its course, how com
pletely he saw through and portrayed the whole sham
more clearly than almost any one in England to-day wi
the thing lying a hopeless wreck before our eyes. So, ap

parently, can even great spirits be seduced by the propaganda-fever under the influence of which they will lay about them with "Thor's hammer," even though they must cease to speak truthfully under the delirium.

"The Individualist" by Alice Groff.

The Individualist (with a great capital "I") is always talking of "*the*" individual. There is no "the" individual. There are individuals - whose name is legion - but among these each is only "*an*" individual.

The individualist is always thinking of a grown-up individual - and pre-eminently of himself as this individual - and as having been born such an individual. He confounds individuality with personality. He seems unable to realise that each individual is born a *child* - capable of being trained into anything within the limits of its specialised race heritage - the heritage of vertical evolution; seems unable to realise that the only invincible heredity is that of the type - that personality is entirely the outcome of environment - horizontal evolution.

Thus the individualist is seen to live in chimera, wherein is no reality.

Max Stirner's greatness, as a supreme individualist, lay only in the colossal poetic imagination which was his specialised race heritage and which his personality perverted into an attempt to envelop the cosmos in chimera.

The New Freewoman

Vol. 1, No. 12 (December 1 1913), pg. 239

Advertisement. Uncredited.

Repeated in *The New Freewoman*:

Vol. 1, No. 13 (December 15 1913) p. 260
Vol. 2, No. 1 (January 1 1914) p. 20

The New Freewoman

Vol. 1, No. 13 (December 15 1913), pg. 254 - 255, 259, 260

"Lego et Penso" by Benjamin R. Tucker.

If a first point was gained, in my little tilt with Miss Marsden, in causing her to offset her too flattering remarks about Americans by an estimate of them apparently belittling, a second point now is gained in causing her to express contrition for having momentarily abandoned her Stirnerism to the extent of bunching individuals according to their nationality and ancestry. And I may claim even a third advance in having elicited from her a new appreciation of Proudhon, which, if still inadequate, is at least more generously specific in its allotments to the credit side of that author's long account. But, as to the main contention, - whether it is crazy to think of voluntary co-operation for defence, in conformity with a voluntary contract fixing the limits of such co-operation, as a possibility of the future, - we are no farther forward than before; for Miss Marsden still neglects to supply a reason why a person who pursues that ideal will find his proper environment within the confines of a mad-house. Until such is forthcoming, the discussion cannot proceed.

(The cap, as far as our memory of it goes, was stock size and not intended for Mr. Byington. We prepare one for our correspondent however in the current "Views and Comments" which we hope will sit a little more heavily than the one which he assumed in pure venturesomeness. We likewise commend to him for consideration, M. Bergson's philosophy of ideas of which we are enabled to publish a fragment. Our excuse for having so to do to the translator of Max Stirner, who anticipated Bergson in this domain by more than half a century, is that he appears to ask for it. - ED.)

The Egoist

Vol. 1, No. 2 (January 15 1914), p. 24 – 25

[First of two]

"A Criticism of the Philosophy of Egoism" by Henry Meulen.

> To the Editor of *The Egoist*. MADAM, The sudden chang
> in the title of your journal fills me with misgivings: I wa
> not aware that the Stirnerian Egoism had taken so strong
> hold upon you, and I hasten to beg you to permit me to ex
> plain my disagreement with that philosophy.
>
> Egoism is the doctrine that the motive of every human ac
> tion is the pleasure of the performer, the word "pleasure
> being taken to include all forms of moral satisfaction. Th
> view of orthodoxy to-day is that people sometimes comm
> acts of self-sacrifice. Sometimes I seem to be foregoing
> big "moral" pleasure (a pleasure that, so far as introspec
> tion carries me, I am at that moment appreciating to th
> full) for a smaller, less noble satisfaction; and sometimes
> seem to be sacrificing a strong ignoble pleasure for th
> sake of a weaker noble one. How will you prove to m
> now that in both these cases I am in reality choosing in th
> direction of my greatest pleasure?
>
> It is useless to tell me that the fact of my acting in a partic
> ular way proves the pleasure anticipated from that act t
> have been the stronger: this does but assume the point t
> be proved, for it advances no reason for denying that a
> action may sometimes proceed in the line of the weaker c
> two anticipated pleasures.
>
> It is equally useless to tell me that the fact of my wantin
> to perform an act is a proof that I anticipate the greate
> satisfaction from that course: this again simply assume
> the point at issue, since I, who am surely able more accu
> rately than any outsider to appraise the comparativ

strength of my anticipated pleasures, decide that I want to act in the direction of a weaker pleasure. You will doubtless here assert, as these ingenious Stirnerians do, that the fact of my wanting to perform a particular action A rather than B indicates that there is a greater hunger within me for satisfaction A than for B. Words - mere words. You cannot possibly know my intimate hungers so well as I, and I decide that my hunger for satisfaction A is less than that for B.

The Egoist

Vol. 1, No. 2 (January 15 1914), p. 24 – 25

[Second of two]

"Views and Comments" by Dora Marsden.

Our modesty not withstanding, we protest that we brew our own malt: we are not bottlers and retailers: we are in the wholesale and producing line of business. If our beer bear a resemblance in flavour to other brands, it is due to the similarity of taste in the makers. "Stirnerian" therefore is not the adejective [sic] fittingly to be applied to the egoism of *The Egoist*. What the appropriate term would be we can omit to state. Having said this, we do not seek to minimise the amount of Stirner which may be trace herein. The contrary rather, since having no fear that creative genius folded its wings when Stirner laid down his pen, we would gladly credit to him - unlike so many of the individualists who have enriched themselves somewhat at his hands - the full measure of his astounding creativeness. For it is not the smallness in measure of what one takes away from genius one admires which is creditable. It is a very old story the comedy of discipleship - that though the banquet of wisdom is spread and open to all-comers the number of the foolish abroad does not materially diminish. We may take from where we please, but "how much" depends on how much we can. The wealth of the feast is the affair of the hosts: capacity to take from it concerns only the guest. Since then we recognise his value, why protest that we have drawn at the stream of his creation into thimbles? We take what we can, and our capacity is not measured by thimblefuls. And because it is not, "Stirnerian egoism" has not as Mr. Meulen suggests in the correspondence column "taken such a firm hold" of us. If that appears a paradox to our correspondent we ask him to work it out. It is really very simple and straightforward if he will bear in mind that we are very great pots and can therefore afford to be honest. So few people can.

Der Einsame Nietzsche by Elisabeth Förster-Nietzsche

Leipzig: Alfred Kröner Verlag (1914)

Und noch grösseren Mangel an der Fähigkeit, die Geister zu unterscheiden, verrät es, wenn man Nietzsche mit dem unfreiwilligen Parodisten Fichtes, mit dem Autor des Buches *Der Einzige und sein Eigentum* zusammenstellt - dies aber heisst nichts anderes, als Schriften von fast beispielloser Macht der Rede und einer verhängnisvollen Kraft des Genies mit einer literarischen Kuriosität zusammenstellen.

The Egoist

Vol. 1, No. 3 (February 2 1914), p. 41 - 44

"Men, Machines and Progress" by Dora Marsden.

Marx and Engels (inevitably Mr. |Heinrich| Charle
thinks) faced with the advent of steam-machinery came t
the conclusion that men must of necessity supply them
selves with a new philosophy of living, to wit, one whic
would fit them - men - to the increased dimensions of th
tool. The desire to own things individually must give wa
and adjust itself to collective ownership. Hence Socialis
in all its varieties: Communism, Collectivism, Guildis
which is Syndicalism without its soul; and Syndicalism i
self, of which the soul is anarchistic temper and the bod
of a heavy-footed communism.

All these in his opinion were "moulds of thought" to whic
the minds of thinkers of the 19th century, no matter ho
virile, penetrative and original, must accommodate them
selves, because forsooth the day of the steam engine wa
here. It will not be necessary for us to say that we disagre
entirely with the dictum that a thinker, however great,
unable to think around or away from the mechanistic app
ances of his age, but it is worth pointing out that the 19t
century thinker who preceded Marx provides a direct ref
tation of it. Max Stirner was not hypnotised by the stea
engine. Nor would any thinker who knew his own temp
sufficiently well be capable of exercising a selectio
among the services which his time and age were able to o
fer him. *Das Kapital* was refuted before it was written.

The Journal of Philosophy, Psychology and Scientific Methods

Vol. 11, No. 5 (February 26 1914)

Advertisement for *Nietzsche and Other Exponents of Individualism* by Paul Carus (Chicago: Open Court Publishing 1914).

> [Nietzsche's] predecessor, Max Stirner, and other kindred spirits less known than Nietzsche are introduced, and if the reader adopts the author's views he will condemn the tendencies and thoughts of these erratic philosophers, but at the same time appreciate their aspirations and love them in their very errors.

The Journal of Philosophy, Psychology and Scientific Methods

Vol. 11, No. 6 (March 12 1914)

Advertisement for *Nietzsche and Other Exponents of Individualism* by Paul Carus (Chicago: Open Court Publishing 1914).

> [Nietzsche's] predecessor, Max Stirner, and other kindre- spirits less known than Nietzsche are introduced, and i the reader adopts the author's views he will condemn th tendencies and thoughts of these erratic philosophers, bu at the same time appreciate their aspirations and love ther in their very errors.

The Journal of Philosophy, Psychology and Scientific Methods

Vol. 11, No. 7 (March 26 1914)

Advertisement for *Nietzsche and Other Exponents of Individualism* by Paul Carus (Chicago: Open Court Publishing 1914).

> [Nietzsche's] predecessor, Max Stirner, and other kindre spirits less known than Nietzsche are introduced, and if tl reader adopts the author's views he will condemn the te dencies and thoughts of these erratic philosophers, but the same time appreciate their aspirations and love them i their very errors.

The Journal of Philosophy, Psychology and Scientific Methods

Vol. 11, No. 8 (April 9 1914)

Advertisement for *Nietzsche and Other Exponents of Individualism* by Paul Carus (Chicago: Open Court Publishing 1914).

> [Nietzsche's] predecessor, Max Stirner, and other kindred spirits less known than Nietzsche are introduced, and if the reader adopts the author's views he will condemn the tendencies and thoughts of these erratic philosophers, but at the same time appreciate their aspirations and love them in their very errors.

The Egoist

Vol. 1, No. 8 (April 15 1914), p. 157

"Correspondence" by Dora Marsden.

> We referred Mr. Byington to M. Bergson - who is known even if Stirner is not - in rebuke of the Rip-Van-Winkle tone of astonishment he chose to adopt in criticising our criticism of the present all-powerful vogue of "ideas" in the Platonic sense. That tone has now gone and we welcome its departure, whether resulting from a perusal of Bergson or from some other and unknown cause.

Revue Philosophique de la France et de l'Étranger

T. 78 (July to December 1914), p. 460

Book review of *Nietzsche and Other Exponents of Individualism* by Paul Carus. Review by L. Arréat.

> M. P. C. rappelle fort justement la figure de Max Stirner, ce prédécesseur oublié de Nietzsche; il nomme encore l'Anglais George Moore comme un Nietzsche plus grossier.

The Egoist

Vol. 2, No. 1 (January 1 1915), pg. 4 - 5

"Views and Comments" by Dora Marsden.

> There is a limit to all things. The limit of men's capacity for repeated impressions is very soon reached. Already the war, though as yet it has lasted only six months, has become an institution like the weather. As a dominating Christmas theme even with the Music-Halls it has fallen far short - as far as one has opportunity to judge, that is. Which is hard luck for those who had counted on seeing all the world in the light of a baleful reaction to the Kaiser. We are not all having our heads blown off, not all in trenches or barracks. We are snugly at home: just the same sort of individuals we were before the first of August: requiring to be amused and interested just the same. Hence if anything could arouse one out of the semi-torpor induced by a bad cold, some other things, and the writing of this article, it is the threat to put us all on an intellectual diet of "Thought as thought by the Allies," with pure undiluted English thought as a staple. One might as well become an exile as be compelled to fare off the tepid stewed mush which passes current as thinking to-day in England. The Germans are virile and their virility comes out in their

thinking. Incisive, penetrating, there is the memory of an edge felt somewhere left even when they are dull. And when they are not dull! Stirner was a German, born and buried in Berlin. Of course the English can only gather there was a German Nietzsche: something a little more flashy and possessing considerably less "edge."

The Egoist

Vol. 2, No. 2 (February 1 1915), pg. 31

"A Criticism of *The Egoist*" by Steven T. Byington.

To the Editor, *The Egoist*. MADAM, The expiration of the original guarantee subscriptions makes it opportune to say what one thinks of *The Egoist*, and I yield to the temptation to send some hostile criticisms. [...] Throughout the centuries it has been a familiar cry that the moral code is a device of the dominant classes to confirm their power. Those who raised this cry have never, so far as I remember, been the better intellects; but their error was pardonable in the days before Darwin, when the unanswerable demonstration of the contrary was not in possession of the field of science. To-day pre-Darwinianism of the sort is not pardonable. In this respect I think that Stirner can be admitted as within the sphere of modern thought; *The Egoist*'s editorials cannot.

The Day Book

February 22 1916

"Nietzsche" by Sam Druck.

> I beg leave to explain what Sirfessor Wilkesbarre preaches
> I have had the extreme pleasure of listening to the Sirfes
> sor's lectures and found him to be an excellent expounde
> and popularizer of Max Stirner's and Nietzsche's philoso
> phy. His mode of popularizing these great men's philoso
> phy is by laughing them out of the philosophy of altruism
> and into the consciousness of the ego. For, according t
> Nietzsche, altruism is a slave morality, encouraging sel
> denial and killing self-reliance, and as he postulates tha
> the "I" is older and stronger than the "Thou," by ridiculin
> the egos who have been caught in the trap of slavish altru
> ism, he tends to awaken them to their real importance.

The Egoist

Vol. 2, No. 3 (March 1 1915) pg. 47

"Miss Marsden and the 'I'" by Alice Groff.

> Miss Marsden is holding out hopes also of a possible lat
> realization on her part, that - verbalism aside - "matter an
> spirit," - "subjective and objective" - "the I and the not-I,"
> " the ideal and the real" - "the appearance and the thing-i
> itself" - are simply the result of shifting the psychologic
> centre on the part of the "I" from one pole to the other c
> the battery of life, and that "verbalism" grows out of th
> tendency to put undue emphasis on one pole - at the e
> pense of the other - until finally the "I" is thrown entire
> out of the balance - the polarization of life. Max Stirn
> pushed the emphasis so far toward the subjective - the id

al - the spiritual - the thing-in-itself pole, that he confounded the "I" of the universe and henced eveloped a philosophy of chimera - of madness.

The Egoist

Vol. 2, No. 7 (July 1 1915), pg. 111 – 112

"Passing Paris" by Muriel Ciolkowska.

> This said, *Les Déracinés* stands apart in French and all lit-
> erature, for no book, in the guise of a novel, stirs up things
> to such an extent. M. Maurice Barrés, the arch-individual-
> ist and egoist, who is a personification of the theories of
> Max Stirner, which he has expressed in other forms, has
> gone a step further than Max Stirner, having shown that
> the cult of country and tradition and of all the elements
> which go to the building of the individual and give him his
> grip, are essential fractions - and as such should be glori-
> fied - in the supreme cult of self. Patriotism, heroism, ide-
> alism, esprit de corps give the individual strength and inde-
> pendence and thus form him.

The Day Book

March 9 1916

"Sirfessor Wilkesbarre Will Lecture." Uncredited.

> Sirfessor Wilkesbarre will lecture for the Workers' inst., at
> West Side Auditorium, Taylor and Racine av., 8 pm, Fri.:
> "Can Socialism Save the People." D. Mehlmon will lec-
> ture: "Stirner and Nietzsche," Radical Library, 712 S.
> Loomis, 8pm, Sat.

The Egoist

Vol. 3, No. 3 (March 1 1916), pg. 41 - 43

"The French Word in Modern Prose" by Muriel Ciolkowska.

> |Pierre Jaudon| has read them all, from the classics (whom he quotes too often in their original text) to Stirner, who seems to have impressed him particularly; and they diver him greatly, most of them, as his playful and unpedantic though numerous, quotations show.

The American Journal of Theology

Vol. 22, No. 1 (January 1918), pp. 150-152

Book review of *The Will to Freedom; Or the Gospel of Nietzsche and the Gospel of Christ* by John Neville Figgis. Review by W. C. A. Wallar.

> Dr. Figgis is essentially aristocratic in social theory and thinks almost as little of democracy as Nietzsche himself. An effort appears throughout to reduce the distance between Nietzsche and Christ. As a result of his habit of balancing text against interpretation, his criticism is seldom forthright. Nietzsche's cardinal doctrines are so violently anti-Christian that a task of sophistical jugglery faces a writer who undertakes to make him out a near-Christian. He rejects the common opinion that Nietzsche's ethic is one of pure selfishness, apparently on the ground that the unescapable inconveniences of the selfish life become "sacrificial" when endured for still more selfish supermen! He ascribes to the self-styled anti-Christ remedial criticisms of Christianity to which Nietzsche would never have condescended. He seems anxious to absolve him from "unintentional" consequences. Nietzsche's relation to Kant or to Max Stirner, moreover, is of interest mainly to foot-on-the-fender philosophy-tasters. The public needs plain statement of the fiercest charge the Nietzscheans can make against Christianity and democracy, and then a thoroughgoing demolition of their trenches.

The Journal of English and Germanic Philology

Vol. 17, No. 1 (January 1918), pp. 135-138

Book review of *An Outline of German Romanticism* (Boston: Ginn & Co. 1914) by Allen Wilson Porterfield. Review by Robert H. Fife, Jr.

> It is hard to see why Freiligrath and Herwegh should appear with out Kindel, harder still to understand the omission of Hebel, Gotthelf, Auerbach, Bettina Brentano, Max Stirner and the Graf von Schack, each of whom has certainly a valid title to admission to any work that treats of the fringes of romanticism.

Modern Philology

Vol. 15, No. 10 (February 1918), pp. 603-619

"Auerbach and Nietzsche" by Allen Wilson Porterfield.

> [In *Nietzsche* by Richard M. Meyer,] Meyer lists (pp. 79-97) the following as constituting the most important predecessors of Nietzsche - as his "*verwandte Naturen*": Carlyle, G. F. Daumer, Eugen Dühring, Emerson, Gustave Flaubert, Goethe, Heinse, Karl Hillebrand, Höderlin, Ibsen, Wilhelm Jordan, Paul de Lagarde, Siegfried Lipiner, Ernest Renan, Ruskin, George Sand, and Max Stirner. That is a formidable galaxy and in view of Meyer's enormous *Belesenheit* would be hazardous to gainsay it. But if we may depend upon the complete index to Nietzsche's works, as compiled in the eighteenth volume of the Macmillan edition, Nietzsche never mentioned the following: Heinse, Ruskin, G

F. Daumer, Max Stirner, Wilhelm Jordan, Paul de Lagarde, and Lipiner.

The Egoist

Vol. 5, No. 4 (April 1918), pg. 63

Advertisement. Uncredited.

> *The Eagle and the Serpent*. Is Might Right? Why Do the Ungodly Prosper? Can Altruism Save the World? These questions are answered with astonishing lucidity in the journal *The Eagle and the Serpent*. Such masters as Bernard Shaw, Kidd, W. T. Stead, A. R. Wallace, Ernest Crosty, Benjamin R. Tucker, etc., deal exhaustively with these fundamental questions. The same journal gives you the boiled-down wisdom and wit and wickedness of Stirner, Nietzsche, Montaigne, Rochefoucauld, Chamfort, Emerson, Thoreau, saving the earnest inquirer after forbidden truth a thousand hours of wearying research. There are only a very few left of the bound file containing the two volumes of *The Eagle and the Serpent*. They will cost you £1. Published by J. B. Barnhill, Washington, D.C., U.S.A. [...] THE EGOIST, Ltd. 23 ADELPHI TERRACE HOUSE, ROBERT STREET, W.C. 2.

The Egoist

Vol. 5, No. 5 (May 1918), pg. 76

Advertisement. Uncredited.

> *The Eagle and the Serpent*. Is Might Right? Why Do
> the Ungodly Prosper? Can Altruism Save the World?
> These questions are answered with astonishing lucid
> ity in the journal *The Eagle and the Serpent*. Such
> masters as Bernard Shaw, Kidd, W. T. Stead, A. R.
> Wallace, Ernest Crosty, Benjamin R. Tucker, etc
> deal exhaustively with these fundamental questions
> The same journal gives you the boiled-down wisdom
> and wit and wickedness of Stirner, Nietzsche, Mon
> taigne, Rochefoucauld, Chamfort, Emerson, Thoreau
> saving the earnest inquirer after forbidden truth
> thousand hours of wearying research. There are only
> a very few left of the bound file containing the two
> volumes of *The Eagle and the Serpent*. They will cost
> you £1. Published by J. B. Barnhill, Washington
> D.C., U.S.A. [...] THE EGOIST, Ltd. 23 ADELPHI
> TERRACE HOUSE, ROBERT STREET, W.C. 2.

The Egoist

Vol. 5, No. 6 (June - July 1918), pg. 88

Advertisement. Uncredited.

> *The Eagle and the Serpent*. Is Might Right? Why Do
> the Ungodly Prosper? Can Altruism Save the World?
> These questions are answered with astonishing lucid
> ity in the journal *The Eagle and the Serpent*. Such
> masters as Bernard Shaw, Kidd, W. T. Stead, A. R.
> Wallace, Ernest Crosty, Benjamin R. Tucker, etc

deal exhaustively with these fundamental questions. The same journal gives you the boiled-down wisdom and wit and wickedness of Stirner, Nietzsche, Montaigne, Rochefoucauld, Chamfort, Emerson, Thoreau, saving the earnest inquirer after forbidden truth a thousand hours of wearying research. There are only a very few left of the bound file containing the two volumes of *The Eagle and the Serpent*. They will cost you £1. Published by J. B. Barnhill, Washington, D.C., U.S.A. [...] THE EGOIST, Ltd. 23 ADELPHI TERRACE HOUSE, ROBERT STREET, W.C. 2.

The American Journal of Theology

Vol. 22, No. 3 (July 1918), pp. 376-394

"The Primary Problem for an Empirical Theology" by A. Clinton Watson.

In Germany, Max Stirner and Bahnsen give the non-metaphysical ethics an utterly individualistic tendency, defending a regardlessly solipsistic morality. Deprived thus of even its social anchorage (which it had in those typical French and English movements), the reaction against the philosophical tradition, with its apparently unsolvable religious and epistemological perplexities, finds a frantic culmination in the Nietzschian demand for a "revaluation of all values."

The Egoist

Vol. 5, No. 7 (August 1918), pg. 100

Advertisement. Uncredited.

> *The Eagle and the Serpent*. Is Might Right? Why Do
> the Ungodly Prosper? Can Altruism Save the World?
> These questions are answered with astonishing lucid-
> ity in the journal *The Eagle and the Serpent*. Such
> masters as Bernard Shaw, Kidd, W. T. Stead, A. R.
> Wallace, Ernest Crosty, Benjamin R. Tucker, etc.
> deal exhaustively with these fundamental questions.
> The same journal gives you the boiled-down wisdom
> and wit and wickedness of Stirner, Nietzsche, Mon-
> taigne, Rochefoucauld, Chamfort, Emerson, Thoreau
> saving the earnest inquirer after forbidden truth a
> thousand hours of wearying research. There are only
> a very few left of the bound file containing the two
> volumes of *The Eagle and the Serpent*. They will cost
> you £1. Published by J. B. Barnhill, Washington
> D.C., U.S.A. [...] THE EGOIST, Ltd. 23 ADELPH
> TERRACE HOUSE, ROBERT STREET, W.C. 2.

The Egoist

Vol. 5, No. 8 (September 1918), pg. 112

Advertisement. Uncredited.

> *The Eagle and the Serpent*. Is Might Right? Why Do
> the Ungodly Prosper? Can Altruism Save the World
> These questions are answered with astonishing lucid
> ity in the journal *The Eagle and the Serpent*. Such
> masters as Bernard Shaw, Kidd, W. T. Stead, A. R
> Wallace, Ernest Crosty, Benjamin R. Tucker, etc.

deal exhaustively with these fundamental questions. The same journal gives you the boiled-down wisdom and wit and wickedness of Stirner, Nietzsche, Montaigne, Rochefoucauld, Chamfort, Emerson, Thoreau, saving the earnest inquirer after forbidden truth a thousand hours of wearying research. There are only a very few left of the bound file containing the two volumes of *The Eagle and the Serpent*. They will cost you £1. Published by J. B. Barnhill, Washington, D.C., U.S.A. [...] THE EGOIST, Ltd. 23 ADELPHI TERRACE HOUSE, ROBERT STREET, W.C. 2.

The Musical Quarterly

Vol. 5, No. 4 (October 1919), pp. 561-577

"Camille Saint-Saëns / A Critical Estimate" by D. C. Parker.

The Gargantuan conceptions of Berlioz, the most notable experiments of Liszt, the emotional climaxes of Wagner and Richard Strauss were possible only to men who allowed themselves the larger liberty and were keenly conscious of their power to reach heights that are commonly held to be out bounds. But truth is a relative thing, and we dare not forget Max Stirner's motto. Without inconsistency the critic may give his benediction to those who hold the two views, because, in the end, the justification of theories about music lies in the practical outcome of them. In any case, you cannot force rules upon a strong creative nature.

The Egoist

Vol. 5, No. 10 (November - December 1918), pg.

Advertisement. Uncredited.

> *The Eagle and the Serpent*. Is Might Right? Why Do the
> Ungodly Prosper? Can Altruism Save the World? These
> questions are answered with astonishing lucidity in the
> journal *The Eagle and the Serpent*. The same journal gives
> you the boiled-down wisdom and wit and wickedness of
> Stirner, Nietzsche, Montaigne, Rochefoucauld, Chamfort,
> Emerson, Thoreau. There are only a very few left of the
> bound file containing the two volumes of *The Eagle and
> the Serpent*. They will cost you 15s. [...] THE EGOIST
> Ltd. 23 ADELPHI TERRACE HOUSE, ROBERT
> STREET, W.C. 2.

Apostol egoizma Maks Shtirner by M. A. Kurchinskiĭ

Petrograd: ИЗА-ВО "ОГНИ" 1920.

The Monist

Vol. 30, No. 2 (April 1920), pp. 311-316

"A Forgotten Philosopher" by Max P. Cushing.

> |Paul-Henri Thiry, Baron d'|Holbach has been credited with influencing Max Stirner, David Strauss, and E. von Hartmann. From time to time one sees his name in socialistic writings, whereas Kropotkin claims him for the anarchists. All this leads one to suspect that an attempt to determine Holbach's influence on this school of thought might be productive of most interesting results.

The Sewanee Review

Vol. 28, No. 2 (April 1920), pp. 139-151

"Nietzsche and the Great War" by George Burman Foster.

> Finally, Nietzsche is often tied up with Max Stirner, who employed the Hegelian dialectic to ridicule Feuerbach's Humanity philosophy and to replace the abstraction Humanity with the concrete individual ego - all this in his famous book, *Der Einzige und sein Egenthum*, a book which became the Bible of the so-called "*Edel-Anarchisten*," with whose leader, Krapotkin, Nietzsche likewise has been associated.

The Harvard Theological Review

Vol. 13, No. 4 (October 1920), pp. 362-389

"Theology and Romanticism" by Herbert L. Stewart

> Carlyle's strange delusion that the German people was to
> become Europe's regenerator in virtue may be met by a far
> more plausible argument that that race was to illustrate in
> turn the diverse excesses of immoralism - first the variety
> which springs from a frantic assertion of the personal ego,
> then the variety which comes from a cringing submission
> to the dominant Reich. If Treitschke was to be the apostle
> of the latter, Max Stirner was the apostle of the former.

Herman Schultheiss: Stirner / Grundlagen zun Verstädnis des Werkes "Der Einzige und sein Eigentum" by Herman Schultheiss

Leipzig: Verlag von Felix Meiner 1922.

The 1906 book with new forwards by the author and by publisher Dr. Richard Dedo.

> Eine wissenschaftliche Behandlung der Gedanken Stirners
> wird sich nicht lediglich an das historische Interesse wer-
> den, sondern vielleicht noch lebhaster das systematische in
> Anspruch nehmen. Denn Starrens Buch, *Der Einzige und
> sein Eigentum* tann ohne eine forgfälitte Grötrennung der
> Egoismusgedanten gar nicht verstanden werden, und wenn
> das, was seit sechzig Jahren für und gegen Stirner
> geschrieben worden ist, Geschwäs ist, so liegt es zum
> grössten Teil daran, dass diese Erörettung fehlt.

The American Journal of Psychology

Vol. 33, No. 3 (July 1922), pp. 445-448

Review of "Allgemeine Untersuchung der zwischensubjektischen Beziehungen bei den neueren deutschen Skeptikern" by E. Berner from *Arch. f. d. ges. Psychologie*. Bd. xlii., Heft I. u. 2. Review uncredited.

> The problem of intersubjective relations has received four typical solutions: the negative or solipsistic (Schubert-Soldern, Keibel, Ziehen); the positive by way of a real external world (Goering, Schubert-Soldern, Schmidt); the positive by way of objective assumption of an external world (Bergmann, Weishaupt, Cornelius); and the sceptical (Heim, Spir, Im. Fichte, Stirner, Nietzsche).

Jahrbücher für Nationalökonomie und Statistik / Journal of Economics and Statistics, Dritte Folge

Vol. 67 (122), No. 5 (1924), pp. 677-678, 809-812

"Uebersicht über die neuesten Publikationen Deutschlands und des Auslandes." Uncredited.

> Smith, Adam, *Der Reichtum der Nationen*. (*Inquiry into the nature and causes of the wealth of nations*.) Nach der Uebersetzung von Max Stirner und der englischen Ausgabe von Cannan 91904). Hrsg. von Heinrich Schmid (Jena). 2 Bde. Bd. 1. 2. Leipzig, Alfred Kröner, 1924. VIII - 428; IV - 570 SS. Gm. 15.-.

"Neuentdeckte Schriften von Karl Marx un Friedrich Engles" by Ernst Drahn.

> Engles veröffentlichte schon früher daraus seinen "Feuerbach" und Bernstein in *den Dokumenten des Sozialismus sub II u. IV* den "Sankt Max" (Stirner). [...] Nach ungefährere Schätzung ist dieser Stirner gewidmete Teil u Umfang nicht geringer als *Der Einzige und sein Eigentum*... In der *deutschen Ideologie* haben sich Marx und Engles aber nicht nur mit Stirner auseinandergesetzt. [..] Die Gesamtheit des Manuskriptes lässt inhaltlich erkennen, dass Marx und Engles die Stirner und Bau wesentlich schärfer kristisierten als Feurerbach, den s "als einen Gegner behandeln, den sie hochschätzen... "

Zeitschrift für die gesamte Staatswissenschaft / Journal of Institutional and Theoretical Economics

Bd. 78, H. 1. (1924), pp. 216-220

"Eingesandte Schriften." Uncredited.

> Kurtschinsky, M.: *Der Apostel des Egoismus / Max Stirner und seine Philosophie der Anarchie*. Aus dem Russischen übersetzt von Gregorv. Glasenapp. Berlin: Prager 1923. 177S.

Zeitschrift für die gesamte Staatswissenschaft / Journal of Institutional and Theoretical Economics

Bd. 79, H. 1. (1925), pp. 16-39

"Die Zukunft Der Deutschen Demokratie" by Leo Wittmayer.

> Da jedoch zufolge der in Weimar ausgerufenen Klassenparität jede der beiden Klassen zwar "hindern," aber keine von ihnen einseitig und eigenmächtig handeln kann, da ferner ohne Einvernehmen unter ihnen der Staat stillsteht, wenn nicht der bösen Weissagung eines Max Stirner preisgegeben ist, und da endlich das Einvernehmenan Bedingungen gebundenist, die dieser Uebergangszeit nur zu häufig fehlen, so lassen sich alle diese Schwierigkeitender deutschen Demokratie auf die Formel bringen, daß sie an dem schweren Zirkelleidet, ihre Ziele zugleichzu Voraussetzungenzu haben, ein Widerspruch, der heute auch schon dem Westen geläufiger wird.

Weltwirtschaftliches Archiv

22. Bd. (1925), pp. 45-52

Book review of *Der Apostel des Egoismus / Max Stirner und seine Philosophie der Anarchie* by M. Kurtschinsky (Berlin: Gregor von Glasenapp 1923) Review by HC.

> Der Verf. (Russe, jetzt Professor an der Universität Dor-
> pat) versucht in eingehender Analyse des Stirnersc'
> Werkes und mit umfassen de Hreranziehung verwandte
> Werke und der Werke über Stirner eine systematisch'
> Darstellung seiner Gedanken zu geben, die ihm über de
> unmittelbaren theoritischen oder politischen Aneignun
> seines extrem-individualistischen Radikalismus (bes. auc'
> in Rußland) vernachlässigt zu sein scheint.

The Slavonic Review

Vol. 4, No. 10 (June 1925), pp. 1-17

"The End of the Renaissance / The Contemporary Crisis of Culture" by N. Berdiayev.

> Neither the work of Nietzsche nor the work of Marx was
> triumph of man. They only convicted humanism of its ill
> sions. After them, all sentimental humanism became ir
> possible, as impossible as the high-flown infatuation wi
> humanitarian ideals, or the native faith in humanism. W
> find the same denial of man in Max Stirner, who also ai
> heavy blows at humanism. The human kingdom (standi
> midway between spirit and nature), the kingdom of se
> sufficing humanism falls to pieces and is conquered; t
> point where it ends becomes visible; the limits of man a
> overstepped. In what is purely human it is impossible
> find a firm foothold.

Annalen der Philosophie und philosophischen Kritik

5. Bd., H. 2 (July 6, 1925), pp. 65-66

"Sozial- und Wirtschafsphilosophie." Book review of *Die Würde der Persönlichkeit und ihre wahrung durch die natürliche Wirtschaftsordnung* by Rolf Engert (Jena: Verlag Die Neue Zeit 1925). Review by B.

> Die kleine Schrift ist als Propagandaschrift zugunsten der freiwirtschaftlichen Bewegung im Sinne Silvio Gesell gedacht und ist aus einem Vortrag hervorgegangen, der auf der ersten freiwirtschaftlichen Jugendtagung im Gedenken an Max Stirner gehalten worden ist.

The Philosophical Review

Vol. 35, Index: Volumes 1-35 (1926), pp. 158-180

Citation of "Max Stirner und Friedrich Nietzsche" by Ernest Albee (i. 661) in *The Philosophical Review Index to Vols. I - XXXV.*

Weltwirtschaftliches Archiv

23. Bd. (1926), pp. 286-290

Book review of *Der Vorfrühling der Anarchie / Ihre historische Entwicklung von den Anfängen bis zum Jahre 1864* by Max Nettlau (Berlin: Beiträg zur Geschichte des Sozialismus, Syndikalismus, Anarchismus 1925). Review uncredited.

> Unter dem Leitgedanken dass sich die anarchische Ide
> immer siegreicher durchsetze, gibt der Verf. eine
> Überblick uber die im Laufe der Weltgeschichte aufge
> tretenen antiautoritären Strömungen vom klassischen A
> tertum bis zur Gründung der Internationale. Um durc
> einige Namen den Gang der Darstellung anzudeuten, seie
> die   Stoiker, Karpokrates, Rabelais, Diderot, Sylva
> Marechal, Burkes,   William Godwin,   Robert Owe
> William Thompson, Josiah Warren, P. J. Proudhon, Mɑ
> Stirner und Bakunin genannt.

The Monist

Vol. 36, No. 2 (April 1926), pp. 311-325

"The Main Tendencies in Contemporary Legal and Political Philosophy in Germany" by S. Bovensiepen.

> [Theoretical anarchism] seeks to dissolve the entire leg
> and political order into merely loose, and always easi
> terminable, associations of free egoists. One might ref
> to a work, well known though in ill repute, by Max Stirn
> (1806 - 1856) on *Der Einzige und sein Eigentum.*

The Eagle and the Serpent

Vol. 1, No. 1 (February 1927)

"Editorial." Richard McKnight.

The original *Eagle and Serpent* was published in London from 1898 to 1902. It was created and edited by one of Nature's noblemen, John Erwin McCall. "A Journal of Egoistic Philosophy and Sociology" - that was the old, up-and-fighting *Eagle and Serpent*. It was probably the most unique and daring publication in in the world at that time. It had for its special desideratum the propagation of the philosophy of Nietzsche. Concomitantly, it espoused the ethics and sociology of Montaigne, Stirner, Emerson, Stendhal, La Rochefoucauld, Thoreau, Ibsen, and other representatives of the individualistic school of thought.

"Right, 'Right' for the Individual" by J. L. Walker.

To the intelligent Egoist [Right and Wrong] are two words generally perverted from their meaning and used as scare-crows. There is a frequent clash between the right of one and the right of another, and they fight it out. It is settled by the triumph of one and the defeat of the other. Max Stirner in his matchless book, *The Ego and His Own*, says: *Ist es mir recht, so is es recht* (if it suits me, it is right).

"Egographs." Uncredited.

If it be right for me, it is right. - Stirner

And will you not by these brilliant examples learn that the egoist gets on best? I for my part take a lesson from them, and propose, instead of further unselfishly serving those great egoists, rather to be the egoist myself. - Stirner.

The Gospel According to Malfew Seklew by Malfew Seklew

Chicago: F. M. Wilkesbarr 1927

"The discoverer of a Great Truth well knows that it may be useful to other men, and, as a greedy withholding would bring him no enjoyment, he communicates it." - Max Stirner. [...] "I use the term Egoism, like Stirner, for acts of normal self-possession and self-expression, excluding blind crazes, fanaticism, the influence of fixed ideas, hypnotism dominating the subject and rendering him more of an automaton than an individual, although he goes through the motions. Rewards and punishments, promised and threatened, appeal to the Egoism of ignorant believers, but there is also an anti-individualistic craze or fascination in religion, and love and business, when the idea rides the man. In the last analysis it is a question of sanity or insanity." [...] I am not an Ego along with other Egoes, but the Sole Ego; I am unique! - Max Stirner. [...] "God and mankind have concerned themselves for nothing, for nothing but themselves. Let me then, likewise, concern myself for myself, who am equally with God the nothing of all others, who am my all, who am the only one." - M. Stirner.

Read: Stirner's *The Ego and his Own*.

Archiv für Rechts- und Wirtschaft-sphilosophie

Vol. 20, No. 4 (July 1927), pp. 608-609

"Verhandlungen des 5. Preussischen Richtertags und der Vertreterversammiung des Preussischen Richtervereins zu Kassel am 10. u. 11. Oktober 1926" by Bovensiepen.

Als Neukantianer und Shüler Rudolf Stammlers von einem erkenntinis-kritischen Idealismums ausgehend, nimmt er insbesondere zu den drei grossen Hauptrichtungen der Verneinnung des "Rechts des Rechtes" Stellung, nämlich dem Anarchismus des Max Stirner, *Der Einzige und sein Eigentum*, der die Begründbarkeit sittlicher Werturteile überhaupt leugnet, sodann zu der "pazifistischen" Lehre, wie sie insbesondere Leo Tolstoi vertritt, dass der Staat sittlich nich berechtigt sei, Rechtszang auszuüben, und endlich zu der "soziallistische-kommunistischen Lehre der Verwerflichkeit des Privateigentums" überhaupt.

BLAKE

Jahrbücher für Nationalökonomie und Statistik / Journal of Economics and Statistics, Dritte Folge

Vol. 74 (129), No. 5 (1928), pp. 761-762

"Uebersicht über die neuesten Publikationen Deutschlands und des Auslandes" by Theo Surányi-Unger.

> Macchiavelli, Rousseau, Adam Smith, die deutsche Stürmer und Dränger, Wilhelm von Humboldt, das Jung Deutschland, Schopenhauer, Max Stirner und Nietzsch stellt B. als die Träger dieser Entwicklung hin. [...] ebens könnte man etwa wünschen, dass neben Max Stirner auc dem auf Condorcet zurückgehenden entwicklungsthe retischen Anarchismus Proudhons einige Aufmerksamke geschenkt würde.

Revue d'histoire économique et sociale

Vol. 16, No. 4 (1928), pp. 821-822

Book review of *Les doctrines politiques des philosophes classiques de l'Allemagne* by Victor Basch (Paris; Felix Alcan 1927). Review by Edmond Laskine.

> M. Victor Basch, dont les livres sur l'Esthétique de Kant, sur la poétique de Schiller, sur l'individualisme de Max Stirner sont classiques, a commencé cet ouvrage sur les doctrines politiques des grands philosophes de l'Allemagne pendant la guerre.

Zeitschrift für Theologie und Kirche, Neue Folge

Vol. 9 (36), No. 2 (1928), pp. 81-98

"Philosophischer und religiöser Wirklichkeitsbegriff. Theodor v. Häring zum achtzigsten Geburtstag" by Friedrich Traub.

> Solus ipse - das Ich, das Selbst, das einzig Wirkliche, alles andere, auch die fremden Iche, nur von mir gehegte Vorstellungen. Ein Vertreter dieses Standpunkts war Max Stirner mit seinem Buch: *Der Einzige und sein Eigentum*.

Zeitschrift für Theologie und Kirche, Neue Folge

Vol. 11 (38), No. 5 (1930), pp. 325-338

"Ontologie und Theologie" by Karl Heim.

> Diese Fragestellung, die vom einsamen Ich als dem Urda⬛
> tum ausgeht, beherrscht die ganze Entwicklung de⬛
> Denkens von Cartestus bis zum letzten Ausläufer des Ide⬛
> alismus, der die kartesianisch Boraussetzung noch ein m⬛
> bis in alle und ver ihre erfenntnistheoretischen und ethi⬛
> chen Knonsequenzen folgt hat, Max Stirner.

Revue de Métaphysique et de Morale

T. 37, No. 2 (April to June 1930), p. 8

Book review of *Stirner als Soziolog* by Hans
Sveistrup (Berlin: Struppe et Winckler 1928). Review uncredited.

> M a x Stirner est, comme l'on sait, l'auteur d'un liv⬛
> célèbre: *Der Einzige und sein Eigentum* (*L'unique et s*⬛
> *propriété*), généralement considéré comme un manu⬛
> d'exotisme. On a vu en Stirner le théoricien d'un individ⬛
> alisme anarchique tendant a rendre impossible toute s⬛
> ciété humaine.

Rivista di Filosofia Neo-Scolastica

Vol. 22, No. 6 (November to December 1930), pp. 462- 481

"I Fondamenti Dell'oggettivismo" by Michele Losac-
co.

> Spinto poi all'estreme conseguenze, nel senso che il
> soggetto debba assorbire e identificare a se l'oggetto, "cede
> il posto all'Io concreto reale, il quale effettivamente pensa;
> dal trascendentalismso si passa all'egocentrismo, all'ego-
> tismo, all'Unico stirnerian." (Egli si arresta molto a
> confutare Max Stirner, che fu un individualista paradossale
> anziche un filosofo rigoroso.)

BLAKE

Zeitschrift für Theologie und Kirche, Neue Folge

Vol. 13 (40), No. 3 (1932), pp. 244-268

"Zur Philosophie und Religion des deutschen Idealismus. (S. zuletzt ZThK 1930, Heft 4, S. 299-321.)"
by Rudolf Paulus.

Den Gesamtdarstellungen reiht sichwürdig an die vo-
Moog. Er faßt die Hegelforschung der früheren Zeit un-
der letzten Jahre übersichtlich zusammen, berichet einge-
hend überHegels Werden, gibtin genauem Anschluß an di-
Quellenneinennvorzüglich einführenden Bericht über de-
Gedankengang der Hauptwerke, zum Schluß aus 80 Sei-
eneine über "die Hegelsch Sechule und ihre Gegner," e-
heute wegen Feuerbach, Marx usw. besonders aktuell-
Kapitel (s. z. B. S. 467 Max Stirner über Hegel und d-
Prinzip des Luthertums).

Benjamin R. Tucker

The German Ideology by Karl Marx and Friedrich Engels

Moscow: Marx-Engels Institute 1932

The man who "has based his cause on nothing" begins hi
lengthy "critical hurrah" like a good German, straightwa
with a Jeremiad: "Is there anything that is not to be m
cause?" (p. 5 of the "book"). And he continues lamentin
heart-rendingly that "everything is to be his cause", tha
"God's cause, the cause of mankind, of truth and freedom
and in addition the cause of his people, of his lord", an
thousands of other good causes, are imposed on him. Po(
fellow! The French and English bourgeois complain abo
lack of markets, trade crises, panic on the stock exchang
the political situation prevailing at the moment, etc.; th
German petty bourgeois, whose active participation in th
bourgeois movement has been merely an ideal one, ar
who for the rest exposed only himself to risk, sees his ov
cause simply as the "good cause", the "cause of freedor
truth, mankind", etc. Our German school-teacher simp
believes this illusion of the German petty bourgeois and c
three pages he provisionally discusses all these good cau
on. He investigates "God's cause", "the cause
mankind" (pp. 6 and 7) and finds these are "purely egoist
cal causes", that both "God" and "mankind" worry on
about what is theirs, that "truth, freedom, humanity, ju
tice" are "only interested in themselves and not in us, on
in their own well-being and not in ours" - from which
concludes that all these persons "are thereby exceptional
well-off." He goes so far as to transform these idealis
phrases - God, truth, etc. - into prosperous burghers w
"are exceptionally well-off" and enjoy a "profitable eg
ism". But this vexes the holy egoist: "And I?" he exclaim
"I, for my part, draw the lesson from this and, instead
continuing to serve these great egoists, I should rather
an egoist myself!" (p. 7) Thus we see what holy motiv
guide Saint Max in his transition to egoism. It is not t
good things of this world, not treasures which moth a
rust corrupt, not the capital belonging to his fellow uniq

ones, but heavenly treasure, the capital which belongs to God, truth, freedom, mankind, etc., that gives him no peace.

Social Science

Vol. 7, No. 1 (January 1932), pp. 50-57

"Materialism" by Marcellus D. R. von Redlich.

Max Stirner was another writer in advocacy of material-ism; he rejected everything transcending the particular Ego and its self-will.

Hispania

Vol. 15, No. 1 (February 1932), pp. 15-24

"Concerning the Ideology of Pío Baroja" by Arthur L. Owen.

> His first three volumes show this lack of orientation mos[t] plainly. Sometime before the writing of *Camino de perfec[-] cion* (1902), he formed a lasting friendship with a Germa[n] Swiss named Paul Schmitz, who introduced him to th[e] philosophical thought of Germany, where, particularly i[n] the work of Max Stirner, Schopenhauer, and Nietzsche, h[e] found, stated clearly and scientifically, problems which h[e] had set for himself in a defective and obscure fashion. I[n] other and more personal ways, also, Schmitz did much [to] further Baroja's slow and painful spiritual development.

Historische Zeitschrift. Beihefte, Vol. 31, Rudolf Haym und die Anfänge des klassischen Liberalismus

(1933), pp. 1-3, 5, 7, 9-208

"Rudolf Haym und die Anfänge des klassischen Liberalismus" by Hans Rosenberg.

> D a s s Feuerbach in so starkem Masse auf sei[ne] Zeitgenossen und insbesondere auf den Werdegang höch[st] verschiedenartiger, hochbegabter Köpfe gewirkt hat - sie nur an seinen entscheidenden Einfluss auf die Entwic[k] lung von Karl Marx, Friedrich Engels, Moses Hess, M[ax] Stirner |…| eklärt sich vor allem daraus dass er innerha[lb] der philosophischen Bewegung der 1840er Jahre d[er] einzige wahrhaft originale, schöpferische Kopf war.

Revue Philosophique de la France et de l'Étranger

T. 116 (July to December 1933), pp. 28-49

"Ce qui est vivant et ce qui est mort dans le matérialisme" by R. Ruyer.

> La science, remarque Bachelard, on croyait autrefois qu'elle "était réelle par ses objets, hypothétique par les liaison établies entreles" - absolument, peut-on ajouter, comme le matérialiste Max Stirner niait la réalité de la société, parce qu'elle n'a pas de corps comme l'individu - mais "ce sont maintenant les objets qui sont representes par des metaphores, et c'est leur organisation qui fait figure de réalité."

International Journal of Ethics

Vol. 44, No. 1 (October 1933), pp. 106-128

"Oughtness and Order" by T. V. Smith.

> It is incorrigibly the judge from a vantage where it, save *ex post facto*, is not among the judged. It could not be itself and surrender this prerogative. With Max Stirner, it must cry that "nothing is more to me than myself." The mystery of conscience is not, then, in its claim for special privilege, its drive for power; that is the nature of life from elemental spontaneity to final duty dictation. "God and mankind," says Stirner again,"have concerned themselves for nothing, for nothing but themselves. Let me then likewise concern myself for myself, who am equally with God the nothing of all others, who am my all, who am the only one." The mystery of conscience, if such there be, is in its altruistic streak, its trying to renounce the superiority of judging for the equalitarianism which is judged.

Isis

Vol. 20, No. 2 (January 1934), pp. 506-626

Book review of *Le desir du neant. Contribution a la psychologie du divertissement* (Bibl. de philosophie contemporaine) by Louis Vialle (Paris: Alcan 1933) Review by L. Guinet.

> Enfin, la redemption individualiste, qui peut se revetir de formes tres variees, est presentee avec les exemples de F P. DE SENANCOUR (dont le nom, on ne sait pourquoi n'est pas prononce dans les pages qui lui sont consacrees de A. DE VIGNY, de H. F. AMIEL, et surtout de MA STIRNER.

The American Magazine of Art

Vol. 27, No. 11 (November 1934), pp. 577-579

"On Sound Painting and Other Incidentals" by Guy Pénc du Bois.

Any canvas that has gone on or is expected to go on for cen turies must have a life of its own. It must be sound in th sense. There is no other sense in which any real thing can be considered sound. It would be most extraordinary if this cou remain unforgotten. Soundness in the artist is certainly n comparable to soundness in the banker. The latter's consis merely in living within the limits of a prescribed code morals or, as Max Stirner would have it, in living the life of ghost. The artist can be neither so restricted nor so empty. H work certainly can have nothing to do with codes. It is sou because it is alive, because it contains the heart and soul a thought of an independent personality and is itself within own frame a living thing.

Archiv für Rechts- und Sozialphilosophie

Vol. 29, No. 1 (October 1935), pp. 29-52

"Die Untrennbarkeit von Sittlichkeit und Recht" by Hermann Roeder.

> Ähnlich bildet auch bei Nietzsche im Anklang an Gedanken des Anarchisten Max Stirner der Staat - "das kälteste aller Ungeheuer," wie er ihn in seinem Hauptwerke *Also sprach Zarathustra* mennt.

Political Science Quarterly

Vol. 50, No. 4 (December 1935), pp. 525-560

"Individual, State and Corporation" by Giorgio Del Vecchio.

> Perhaps we can at times recognize some aesthetic or literary value in the expressions of extreme individualism, as for example in those of Stirner: "Individual will and the State are powers in mortal enmity to each other, between them there is no possibility of any 'perpetual peace.'" "The State always aims only at limiting the individual, subordinating and subjecting him to any generality whatever; it only lasts till the individual becomes an integral part, and is nothing but the clearly expressed limitation of the ego, it is my limitation, my slavery." "For this reason the State and I are enemies." "The State is founded on the slavery of work. From the moment work becomes free the State is lost." Max Stirner, *Der Einzige und sein Eigentum* (ed. Reclam), p. 228.

Synthese

Vol. 1, No. 10 (1936), pp. 300-308

"'Der Einzige' und 'Der Einzelne' (Ueber Stirner und Kierkegaard)" by Martin Buber.

> Wenige Jahre, ehe Kierkegaard unter dem Titel *De Gesichtspunkt fur meine Wirksamkeit als Schriftstelle* seinen "Rapport an die Geschichte" entwarf, in desse "Beilagen" die Kategorie des Einzelnen ihre zureichend Formulierung fand, verfasste Max Stirner sein Buch ube den *Einzigen*.

American Journal of Sociology

Vol. 41, No. 4 (January 1936), pp. 470-483

"Philosophical Anarchism: Its Rise, Decline and Eclipse" by Victor S. Yarros.

> |Benjamin| Tucker's economic and political views re mained essentially the same throughout his career as anarchistic editor, teacher and writer. But his ethical ar philosophical ideas, rather unfortunately, were complete revolutionized by "Max Stirner," or Caspar Schmidt, th German pedagogue and author of a single book, *D Einzige und sein Eigenthum* - available in an Engli translation under the title, *The Ego and His Own*, Tuck was introduced to this volume by John Henry Mackay, t Scotch-German poet and novelist, whom Tucker had co verted to anarchism. He repudiated the ideas of t philosophers of social and moral evolution. The individ al or ego, he argued, owed no allegiance to anyone. H was supreme, and, if intelligent, governed himself entire by utilitarian considerations. He might or might not c operate with others; self-interest and expediency were h only guides. A society composed of conscious egois

would be based on contract, and on nothing else. There would be nothing mystical or supernatural about it. Men want peace, and peace can be achieved by discussion and agreement. Altruism was nonsense, a figment of the romantic imagination. All men are selfish, but selfishness assumes different forms and manifestations. It is selfish to please one's self; it is just as selfish to please others whom one likes to please, or whom one loves; it is selfish to devote one's life and abilities to a cause; it is selfish to give up one's life for an ideal. One's kind of selfishness is determined by environment, by books, by accident, by tempermental traits. But no selfishness is "higher" than any other selfishness. [...] This pseudo-realistic gospel irritated and alienated those of Tucker's followers who had come to him via Spencer and who accepted evolutionary ethics. It also offended the few sincerely religious Christians who saw no conflict between the teachings of Jesus and pacific and democratic anarchism. The movement was bound to suffer from these losses. It could not but be adversely effected, too, by the emerging school of social psychology, which made hash of Stirner's arbitrary and verbal distinctions.

The American Political Science Review

Vol. 30, No. 4 (August 1936), pp. 653-680

"The Legal Meaning of the Pact for the Renunciation of War" by Miroslas Gonsiorowski.

[Discussing the Pact of Paris] It has been contended that such an idea is false, and that to prevent the natural development of strong states by supporting the weak ones is a sorry service to peace and stability. This opinion is surprisingly akin to that of a theoretical founder of anarchism, Max Stirner, who said: "He who has force has right, he who has no force has no right."

Vierteljahrschrift für Sozial- und Wirtschaftsgeschichtes

30. Bd., H. 4 (1937), pp. 313- 346

"Volkswirtschaft und Weltwirtschaft im deutschen Merkantilismus" by Anton Tautscher mentions *Der Reichtum der Nationen* by Adam Smith, translated by Stirner.

> "Wie bei einem reichen Manne hält man auch ein reiche
> Land für ein solches, welches Geld im Überfluss hat. Gol
> und Silber in einem Lande anzuhäufen, denkt man sieh a
> den einfachsten Weg, es zu bereichern" (A. Smith, *De*
> *Reichtum der Nationen*. Deutsche von Max Stirner, 192
> Bd. 2, S. 2.).

The Journal of Philosophy

Vol. 34, No. 2 (January 21 1937), pp. 47-49

Book review of *From Hegel to Marx* by Sidney Hook (New York: Reynal and Hitchcock 1936). Re view by VJMcG.

> This book is a welcome contribution to a field of studi
> unfortunately, though not inexplicably, much neglected I
> American scholars. It constitutes, in fact, one of the first a
> tempts in English to expound in detail the series
> thinkers: Bruno Bauer, Arnold Ruge, Max Stirner, Mos
> Hess, Ludwig Feuerbach, and others, against whose br
> liance and shortcomings, whether in opposition or agre
> ment, young Marx hammered out his own more formidal
> and persistent theory.

The American Economic Review

Vol. 27, No. 1 (March 1937), pp. 119-124

Book review of *From Hegel to Marx* by Sidney
Hook by Sidney Hook (New York: Reynal and
Hitchcock 1936). Review by George M. Janes.

> Sidney Hook is associate professor of philosophy at New
> York University and has already written a book on Marx.
> In this volume he discusses the intellectual development of
> Karl Marx in eight chapters: (1) Hegel and Marx; (2) The
> young-Hegelians and Karl Marx; (3) Bruno Bauer and
> Karl Marx; (4) Arnold Ruge and Karl Marx; (5) Max
> Stirner and Karl Marx; (6) Moses Hess and Karl Marx; (7)
> Ludwig Feuerbachand Karl Marx; (8) Karl Marx and
> Feuerbach.

International Journal of Ethics

Vol. 47, No. 3 (April 1937), pp. 405-406

Book review of *From Hegel to Marx* by Sidney
Hook (New York: Reynal and Hitchcock 1936).
Review by Harold D. Lasswell.

> No doubt the historian of political philosophy will wel-
> come the discussion of Marx's neglected analysis of Max
> Stirner. […] Indeed, if one interrelationship stands out
> above the rest, it is the debt of Marx (and of social critics
> generally) to the spirit, and especially the method, of those
> scholars who were revolutionizing the attitude of modern
> thinkers toward ecclesiastical forms and dogmas.

The Modern Language Journal

Vol. 22, No. 4 (January 1938), pp. 250-264

"Deutsche Gedenktage / A Calendar for the German Language Club" by Bayard Q. Morgan and Stella M. Hinz.

> As the sub-title implies, the chief purpose in presenting the material contained in the appended list is to assist the teacher in providing suitable programs for the language club. Suppose the teacher needs an idea for the March meeting of the German club. Turning to this calendar, he will note that Goethe died on March 22. Good, let us celebrate the anniversary of Goethe's death. [...] October 2° 1806: born, Max Max Stirner, philosopher. [...] June 2° 1856. died, Max Stirner, philosopher.

The Philosophical Review

Vol. 47, No. 2 (March 1938), pp. 218-221

Book review of *From Hegel to Marx* by Sidney Hook (New York: Reynal and Hitchcock 1936). Review by George H. Sabine.

> The historical studies included in the volume deal chiefly with David Friedrich Strauss, Bruno Bauer, Arnold Ruge Max Stirner, Moses Hess, and Ludwig Feuerbach. They offer a careful analysis of the climate of opinion with which Marx first stated his philosophy and of the many intellectual motives, some congenial and some antagonistic with reference to which he shaped his own ideas.

Books Abroad

Vol. 12, No. 2 (Spring 1938), p. 216

Book review of *Die Philosophic Max Stirners im Gegensatz zum Hegelschen Idealismus* by Kurt Adolf Mautz (1936). Review by Bonno Tapper.

> Stirner's philosophy or better mythology of "the natural man" (see especially *Der Einzige und sein Eigentum*: the Only One and his Property) is directed against Hegel's philosophy of *Spirit and History*.

Archiv für Rechts- und Sozialphilosophie

Vol. 33 (1939 to 1940), pp. 56-148

"Kernprobleme der Rechtsphilosophie" by Alexander Graf zu Dohna.

> An den äussersten Enden der Reihe stehen sich, gewissermassen als Antipoden, Leo Tolstoi und Max Stirner gegenüber. […] Damit vergleiche man die Sprache, in der Max Stirner sich gefällt, "Ob, was Ich denke und tue, christlich sei, was kümmert das Mich?" […] Trotz des Abgrundes, der hiernach die beiden Männer scheidet, finden sie sich doch zusammen in der Ablehnung de Staates, an dessen Stelle Stirner den Verein der Egoisten, Tolstoi die Gemeinschaft einander liebender und dienender Menschen setzen möchte. "Ich bin der Todfeind des Staates," erklärt Stirner. […] Als Mittel aber, mit dem die Staatsmacht gebrochen werden soll, dekt Stirner sich die nackte Gewalt, Tolstoi dagegen die entwaffnende Wahrhaftigkeit. […] So Stirner; dagegen Tolstoi: "Wollten wir nur aufhören zu lügen und uns zu stellen, als ob wir die Wahrheit nicht sähen, wollten wir nur für die Wahrheit... "

The Review of Politics

Vol. 1, No. 3 (July 1939), pp. 261-274

"Limes Germanicus / Bridge and Frontier Part One" by Goetz A. Briefs.

> L. von Stein, the great disciple of Hegel, formulated as human characteristic what is rather characteristic for German type: "In each individual there lives an insupera ble urge toward a perfect domination over the outward ex istence, toward the full possession of all spiritual (menta intellectual) and material goods." We omit citing the fir cry of subjectivistic dynamism represented by Max Stirne and Friedrich Nietzsche.

Jewish Social Studies

Vol. 1, No. 4 (October 1939), pp. 409-422

"Early German Socialism and Jewish Emancipa- tion" by Gustav Mayer.

> The Young Hegelians had considered themselves t "thunder legion of the state." Now they thought of then selves as an *ecclesia pressa*. Soon the most radical amoı them began to express doubts not only concerning religi but also concerning the idea of the state. They wondere whether it would be sufficient merely to secularize t state or whether the onward pulsing pressure of the spi of the age would not dispose of the state altogether. It w out of such doubts that Max Stirner, Edgar Bauer and Lu wig Buhl turned to anarchism, while Friedrich Engels fo lowed by Karl Marx, turned to communism.

Revista Mexicana de Sociología

Vol. 1, No. 4/5 (September to December 1939), pp. 65-98

"La Tipología Constructiva en las Ciencias Sociales" by Howard Becker.

> Eigentlich ha sido traducido por "real" y peculiar porque no hay otra expresion mis adecuada. Si Ranke hubiera dicho simplemente wirklich, entonces "real" hubiera sido suficiente, pero eigentlich es otra cosa. Eigen quiere decir "propio"; eigentumlich quiere decir "original" o "peculiar"; Eigentum quiere decir "propiedad" o "atributo", como en la obra de Max Stirner *Des Einzigo und Sein Eigentum* generalmente traducido por *The Ego and His Own*, (*El Ego y lo Suyo*).

Journal of the History of Ideas

Vol. 1, No. 2 (April 1940), pp. 131-150

"The National Socialists' Use of Nietzsche" by
Crane Brinton.

> Baeumler's point-by-point analysis is, however, his reall
> great achievement. Nietzsche, for instance, wrote a grea
> deal that seems on the surface to be the kind of individual
> ism, even anarchism, popular with the superior aestheti
> souls of the late nineteenth century. Nietzsche has even, b
> unenlightened critics, been coupled with Max Stirner, th
> author of *The Ego and Its Own*. Certainly one of the thing
> Mr. H. L. Mencken and Mr. G. B. Shaw found to admir
> in Nietzsche was this insistence that really strong men a
> not to be tied down to any sentimental identification
> themselves with the state, or with society, or with any oth
> er group composed largely of stupid men. Now in the Na
> state, individualism, anarchism, distrust of the state, a
> forbidden doctrines. Baeumler feels that he has to sho
> that Nietzsche *under proper conditions* would have ident
> fied himself as whole-heartedly with the state as does ar
> good brownshirt.

The Journal of Politics

Vol. 2, No. 3 (August 1940), pp. 343-344

Book review of *The Story of the Political Philosophers* by George Calin (New York: McGraw-Hill Book Company 1939). Review by Cortez A. M. Ewing.

> Catlin's discussion of anarchism is quite unsatisfactory. Small mention is made of William Godwin. Bakunin is placed before Proudhon, and the latter is considered in relation with Karl Marx, with whom he could agree only as to their mutual opposition to the existing politico-economic order. But political theories are doctrines of solution and not of immediate tactics. Tolstoy and Kropotkin receive sufficient notice; but Max Stirner is skimped, and the American anarchists are painfully omitted except for Henry Thoreau, who certainly ought not to be considered in the company of a Proudhon. Skepticism is not synonymous with anarchism.

Historische Zeitschrift

Bd. 164, H. 1 (1941), pp. 102-113

"Zur Geschichte der Judenfrage" by Walter Frank.

> Es gehört vielmehr die geistige Auseinandersetzung in der Hegelschen Linken hinzu, die im Gegensatz zu Marx und Lassalle von Bruno Bauer, Ludwig Feuerbach und Max Stirner zu Eugen Dürings Begründung eines sozialistischen Rassenantisemitismus führt.

The Journal of Politics

Vol. 3, No. 2 (May 1941), pp. 133-153

"Leadership: Institutional and Personal" by Sigmund Neumann.

As a matter of fact, the dictator is usually an unsociable individualist by nature. Young Mussolini, brought up in the smithy of his Anarcho-socialist father and the group of his political cronies, was a restless, pugnacious, combative and domineering type of a fellow. He certainly honored though in a very Romanesque way, Benito Juarez, the Mexican revolutionary after whom he was named. There are tales of stone-throwing fights similar to stories told of Napoleon. Of course many other boys threw stones. Young Mussolini did not seem to have been a good mixer. He was an unsociable individualist, and in one of his weak moments he confessed to Emil Ludwig (*Talks with Mussolini*) that Max Stirner, the great theorist of anarchism was his beloved author. There is something to the psychologist's observation that those who do not like to take orders want to give them.

Zeitschrift für Slavische Philologie

Vol. 18, No. 1 (1942), pp. 235-245

Book reviews of *Deutsche Einflüsse auf Pentscho Slawejkoff* by Ewgenij K. Teodoroff (Leipzig: Meiner 1939) and *Die Bedeutung Deutsch- lands für die geistige by ntwicklung Pentscho Slawejkoffs* by Stephka Petrowa (Leipzig: Phil. Diss 1941). Review by Heinrich Jilek.

> Dieser Mensch tragt unzweifelhaft die Zuge von Nietzsche Ubermenschen und Slavejkovs Konzeption reiht sich ein in die Reihe der Ubermenschenphantasien eines Max Stirner, Nietzsche und Dostojevskij.

Journal of the History of Ideas

Vol. 3, No. 2 (April 1942), pp. 159-181

"The Forging of Fascist Doctrine" by Clarence H. Yarrow.

> It is difficult indeed to thread one's way through the tan- gled skein of ideas during this period from the spring of 1919 to the end of 1920. At one time, after his forces had made a very poor showing in the elections to the Chamber of Deputies held in December, 1919, Mussolini came out with strongly anarchistic statements, reminiscent of Max Stirner, an early favorite of his.

Jahrbücher für Nationalökonomie und Statistik / Journal of Economics and Statistics

Vol. 156, No. 6 (December 1942), pp. 464-497

"Zwiespältigkeiten der Lohnlehren" by Adolf Weber

> *Lehrbuch der praktischen Ökonomie*, deutsch von Ma
> Stirner, Leipzig 1845, Bd. III, S. 68.

Historische Zeitschrift

Bd. 167, H. 3 (1943), p. 671

Book review of *Deutschlands Beruf in Gegenwart und Zukunft von Theodor Rohmer* by Alfred Otto Stolze appearing in *Historischen Zeitschrift teilt Bibliotheksrat.* Review uncredited

> Ihr Verfasser ist Max Stirner, bekannt durch sein Buc
> *Der Einzige und sein Eigentum* (1844). In den von Joh
> H e n r y Mackay gesammelten und herausgegebene
> "Kleineren Schriften" Stirners ist die Besprechung nic
> enthalten.

PMLA

Vol. 60, Supplement (1945), pp. 1181-1289

"Germanic Languages and Literatures / Bibliography for 1945 - German" by Henry W. Nordmeyer.

> Mackay. Riley, Thomas A. "New England Anarchism in Germany." NEQ, xv III. 25-38. Critical discussion of John Henry Mackay's novellistic work, exploring his connections with B. R. Tucker, the American anarchist and first "discoverer" of Max Stirner.

Journal of the History of Ideas

Vol. 6, No. 1 (January 1945), pp. 46-66

"Anarchism in the United States" by Charles A. Madison.

Caspar Schmidt, better known as Max Stirner, was at th
same time |as Pierre Joseph Proudhon| developing th
doctrine of egotistical anarchism in his provocative book
The Ego and His Own. Repelled by the sentimentalism c
the utopian socialists as well as by the authoritarianism c
Hegel's absolute state, he stressed the complete supremac
of the individual. He argued that the highest form of civ
lization is predicated upon the assumption that each huma
being is a sovereign unto himself and free to follow hi
own bent. In the process he formulated a philosophy c
egoism which disdained all social and ethical standard
"A fig for good and evil! I am I, and I am neither good n
evil. Neither has any meaning for me... For me there
nothing above myself". Consequently he, as egois
laughed at the claims of others when they conflicted wi
his own needs and desires. His proposed League of Egois
was a utopia of petty *bourgeois* in revolt, and late in th
century attracted a considerable number of romantic bc
hemians. Ironically enough, the hard selfishness of this i
dividualist anarchism was admirably adapted to th
"rugged individualism" of modern capitalism. [...] Be
jamin R. Tucker was the most widely known of the Ame
can individualist anarchists. He was born in 1854 and a
rived at his political philosophy after a study of the wri
ings of Warren, Proudhon, and Stirner.

Revista Portuguesa de Filosofia

T. 1, Fasc. 1 (January to March 1945), pp. 108-110

Book review of *O pensamento alemao de Lutero a Nietzsche* by J. E. Spenle (Coimbra: Armenio Amado 1942). Review by MN.

A doutrina feuerbaquiana suscitou um novo radicalismo, mais avancado nas suas negacoes, representando, no livro de Max Stirner *O unico e a sua propreidade*. [...] O radicalismo filosofico, filiado no teologia hegeliana, atinge, nos seus representantes extremos, tanto no individualismo anarquico de Max Stirner, como na doutrina de Karl Marx, atitudes meramente nilistas.

The Review of Politics

Vol. 7, No. 2 (April 1945), pp. 199-209

"The Prophet of German Nihilism / Ernst Juenger" by Eugene Guerster-Steinhausen.

> A hundred years ago the nihilism of a Max Stirner coul
> wrap itself in the romantic attitude of a private anarchis
> Since then a fundamental change has occurred in ou
> world: the transformation of reality out of the spirit of
> modern technology assuming autonomous powers. Mora
> ists and ideologists may remain bewildered and baffled b
> the extreme possibilities of modern technology; but th
> fearless nihilist seems to be the right man to explore i
> greatest potential. He is fearless in a world which all th
> gods have forsaken for a long time. Nature seems eager
> make him supreme master of this world. Let democra
> and pacifists brood over verbose programs for disarma
> ment - programs which one single audacious chemi
> working in the loneliness of his laboratory can reduce
> scraps of paper in one night! The national nihilist, standir
> squarely upon the biological reality of his own people, ca
> now envisage the extermination of the human race.

The New England Quarterly

Vol. 18, No. 1 (March 1945), pp. 25-38

"New England Anarchism in Germany" by Thomas A. Riley.

> Mackay's real contribution to individualistic anarchism lies however, primarily in the two semi-novels *Die Anarchisten* and *Der Freiheitsuche* [...] In *Die Anarchisten* there are two characters, one of which represents a philosophy of life that is clearly communist-anarchism; the other, a more intellectual person, is an individualistic anarchist and an egoist. Through the eyes of these two men we see the horrors of life among the London poor in 1887 and the useless attempts of London radicals to wipe out the evils of the world by means of an effective social movement. Only by individualism *a la* Tucker and egoism a la Max Stirner can the world progress out of misery, poverty, and wars produced by governments.

BLAKE

CRITICISM

The Eagle and the Serpent

Vol. 2, No. 2 (October 1900)

"John Henry Makay's Appreciation of Stirner." John Mackay. Translated by Thomas Common.

The significance of "The Sole One" is still, as it was fifty years ago, divined and felt rather than known. How could it be otherwise in times when, in fact, everything totters to which we have hitherto clung, when we are zealously striving to replace the old estimates of worth by new ones, when the old stale wine is being again and again poured into new bottles instead of being poured away, and when we are still so little convinced of the absolute worthlessness of most of the estimates of worth!

We are a generation living betwixt night and day. Half awakened, we still rub our somnolent eyes, and are afraid to look into the light.

We cannot separate ourselves from the old abodes of our ideas, although they collapse over our heads; we are too cowardly to forsake the old home and commit ourselves to the sea of self-con-sciousness that can alone bear us to the other shore; we have not yet any genuine confidence in the future, although (or rather because) we have no longer confidence in ourselves.

We no longer believe in God; assuredly it is so. We have become atheists, but we have remained "pious people." We no longer pray in presence of the church bogey; we kneel before the sanctuaries of our heart.

We still get into estatic states as formerly, and the wretchedness of our awakening is the same Only we awake more frequently, and our condition is that of reeling betwixt intoxication and doubt; it is no longer the holy, eternal ecstacy of the first "true Christians.

Then this man comes amongst us.

He does not come with the condescension of the priest - he is not in the service of God, or of an idea whatsoever; nor with the fussiness of the teacher - he leaves us to believe or reject what he says; nor with the anxiety of the physician - he lets us live or die, for he knows that our fancy is our disease. Nor does he come like the philosopher who tries to catch us in the net of a new system of speculation. He despises the philosopher's language, the hideous, obscure, and unintelligible language used as a privilege by those who only want to talk among themselves; he makes for himself a language of his own, for he knows that all knowledge can be intelligible when it wants to be intelligible.

He does not speak of us; he hardly even speaks to us.

He speaks of himself, and always of himself only; and we see how this ego of his strips itself of one fetter after another, until it stands free and unconquerable, in proud self-splendour, as its own master, the last on the field which it has finally won.

It is nothing more nor less than the declaration of the sovereignty of the individual, his incomparability and his uniqueness, that Stirner announces. Hitherto one had only spoken of his rights and duties, and where they begin and end; Stirner, however, er, declares that we are exempt from the latter, and have control over the former. We must make our choice. And since we cannot go back into the night, we must enter into the day.

For we know now that we are all of us egoists. When we survey our actions, we see that some of them have carried us further, much further, than our consciousness wishes to acknowledge, while others have got us entangled in discords quite incapable of being harmonised. Henceforth it will be in vain for us any longer to attempt to deceive ourselves and others concerning the motives of our conduct. Now that we have acknowledged them, what else remains for us but to accommodate ourselves to them?

The result will teach us what we have to thank Stirner for, if the example of those who have so lived their life has not yet shown it to us.

It is our final acknowledgment. Let us no longer stand up against it.

For verily, not too early does the day dawn, after this all-too-long night.

He has raised the bowed head, and put a sword into the languid hand. He has removed our faith and given us certainty.

He has again reminded us of our true interests, of our profane, personal particular-interests, and shown us that it is precisely their pursuit, and not sacrificing ourselves to ideal, sacred and external interests, to the interests of all, that brings back the happiness to life, which we seem to have lost.

Since he has dissected the state of the politi
cian, the society of the socialist and the humanity o
the humanist, and has made it obvious that they
are limitations to our individuality, he has given the
death-blow to all authority - at the same time de
stroying the majority's and collective body's sover
eign will and privilege - and in place of the citizen
the worker, the man, comes the ego, in place of the
incorporeal annihilator, the real creator!

But not that only. Since he devotes the othe
part of his work to the most thorough investigatio
of the conditions under which alone the ego is abl
to develop itself to its uniqueness, he exhibits it t
us in its power, its intercourse, and its self-enjoy
ment - the medium of its force and its final victory.

And in place of our weary, sore-tortured, self-to
menting race, comes the proud, free race of th
"sole ones," to which the future belongs.

He did what he has done for himself, because
was a pleasure to him.

He demands no thanks, and we owe him noth
ing.

He has only reminded us of our indebtedness t
ourselves!

That is what he has done; how he has done it
not less worthy of admiration.

If *originality* and *force* are signs of true geniu
Max Stirner was a genius of the first rank. He see
the world and men entirely with his own eyes, an
everything stands before him in the clearest light
actuality. Nothing can perturb or deceive his pen

trating gaze; neither the night of the past, nor the crowd of desires of his own age. His is an absolutely original work, and there is none that could have been written with more impartiality and freedom from prejudice than "The Sole One and His Prerogative." There is nothing, absolutely nothing, which Stirner accepts as established and given, unless it be his own ego. Nothing bewilders him, confuses him, or imposes on him *a priori*. He thus appears as the genuine child of that critical age, only so infinitely in advance of it, that he begins where the others leave off. This impartiality gives to his words that self-intelligible assurance which so bewilders one person and acts so triumphantly on another.

The *logic* of this thinker is also incomparable. The rigid consistency of his conclusions does not shrink from any, not even from the ultimate consequences. He does not leave it to the reader to extend his thoughts to the limit of their sphere, he does it himself. Conceptions which hitherto appeared unimpugnable, he decomposes one after another, and lets them crumble to dust.

It is not with the outer form of the Christian conception of things, of the rotten, crumbling church of the present day that this battle has to do, but with that spirit which, in ever new forms, continually constructs new strongholds of absolutism, the spirit of Christianity which, like a gloomy vapour, hangs over the past.

It is Stirner's achievement to have divested this spirit of its sanctity, to have unmasked it as the unsubstantial ghost of our imagination. While the most radical thinkers of his age Strauss, Feuerbach and Bauer merely groped with timorous criticism at the conceptions of sanctity, he decomposed them, and allowed them to crumble away.

He vanquishes Christianity in its ultimate conse quences. It is annihilated. It lies behind us with the millennium of its humiliation, the smut of its fraterni ty, the innumerable horrors with which it has stained the page of history, with its falsehood, with its repudiation of all pride, of all individuality, of all genuine pleasure and beauty; and although it sti prevails among us in its final effects, Stirner ha nevertheless removed it from us as a curse!

He stands on the boundary-line between two worlds, and a new epoch in the life of the huma race begins with him - the epoch of freedom.

As yet we have not found any better name for than that of anarchy: the order determined by recip rocal interest, instead of the lack of order under the sway of power which has hitherto prevailed; the ex clusive sovereignty of the individual over his pe sonality, instead of his subjection; his responsibili for his own actions, instead of his tutelage - short, his uniqueness - For it is on the foundation of the Christian view of things that the supports of a those conceptions rest which uphold the sway power; when Stirner has withdrawn the ground from under them, they must fall, and with them falls tha which they have supported.

So violent will be this bloodless and proportio ally rapid-and-sure revolution of all the relations life, that his immortal book will one day be con pared only with the Bible in its wide bearings.

And as this holy book stands at the commenc ment of the Christian era to carry its devastating e

fects for two thousand years into almost the re-
motest corners of the inhabited world, so does the
unholy book of the first self conscious egoist stand
at the entrance to the new age, under the first sign
of which we live, to exercise as blessed an influence as that of the "book of books" was pernicious.

And if we would once more say what it is, how
could we do it better than in its author's own
words? It is this: "A violent, reckless, shameless,
conscienceless, presumptuous - crime" perpetrated
on the sanctity of all authority! And, hailing with joy-
ous shouts the outburst of the purifying, emancipat-
ing storm conjured up by him, we ask with Max
Stirner: "Do not the thunders roll in the distance,
and dost thou not see how the heavens are omi-
nously silent and becoming obscure?"

The North American Review

Vol. 185, No. 616 (June 7 1907), pp. 332-337

Book review of *The Ego and His Own by Max Stirner* (translation by Steven T. Byington. New York:
Benjamin R. Tucker). Review by James Huneker.

What shall it profit a man if he gains the whole
world but loses his own Ego? That is practically the
question put by Max Stirner in his once celebrated,
forgotten and now resuscitated book, *The Ego and
his Own* (*Der Einzige und sein Eigenthum*). Some
one has called man a metaphysical animal; he is either a Platonian or an Aristotelian. Nowadays you
are either a Socialist or an Individualist. You may
not care a straw for either party, yet fate, your temperament and social position, settles the matter
without asking, by your leave. Under which King?
Dr. Butler has spoken of an intellectual aristocracy
and service which is only Nietzscheism attenuated
by slumming; Nietzsche would have naught to do
with such merciful condescension. For him it was
like Brand - All or Nothing. In the Stirner case we
descend into a lower Dantean circle. The Ego is the
frame of the human picture in this airless, sublimat-
ed atmosphere. Yet once breathed, even Nietzsche's mountain top seems thin, rarefied and
bloodless by comparison. Never has the hymn to
Self to the Will been sung in such firm, cool tones;
never logic more infernal - or celestial. (Under
which King?) A homely motto for Stirner might be
Walt Whitman's, "I find no sweeter fat than sticks to
my own bones."

Who is Max Stirner? We knew nothing of him until John Henry Mackay, the Scottish-German rev olutionary poet, dug up his buried book and with it after incalculable pains, a few isolated facts. Stirner was a nickname because of his high forehead; Jo hann Caspar Schmidt was his real name. He was born in Bayreuth, 1806, and died in Berlin, 1856 He had a university education, though he did no distinguish himself, by taking a doctor degree. He taught in a fashionable girls' school, contracted an unhappy marriage, died in poverty and obscurity He met for a decade or so many radical thinkers a a certain circle in Berlin, yet he was more influ enced by the Hegelian philosophy than by the revo lutionary spirit of 1848. He loathed politics. He feared and hated socialism. He was a solitary b nature. Temperament tells in a philosopher as we as a poet. A hesitating, timid man, a sufferer doub less from *aboulia*, as was Amiel, Stirner in his boo (1845) enjoyed a psychic victory over his weaknes of volition. It was the one vigorous affirmation of hi will to live.

For those who love to think of the visible un verse as a cozy corner of God's footstool, there something bleak and terrifying in the isolated posi tion of man since science postulated him as a unimportant bubble on an unimportant planet. The soul shrinks as our conception of outer spac widens. Thomas Hardy describes the sensation a "ghastly." There is said to be no purpose, no desig in all the gleaming phantasmagoria revealed by th astronomer's glass; while on our globe we are brother to lizards, bacteria furnish our motor forc and our brain is but a subtly fashioned mirror, com posed of neuronic filaments, a sort of "dark roor in which is pictured the life without. Well, we adm for the sake of the argument, that we banish God from the firmament, substituting a superior mechanism; we admit our descent from plasma and ascidian worms, we know that we have no free will, because man, like the unicellular organisms, "gives to every stimulus without an inevitable response." That, of course, settles all moral obligations. But we had hoped, we of the old sentimental brigade, that all things being thus adjusted we could live with our fellow man in (comparative) peace, cheating him only in a legitimate business way, and loving our neighbor better than ourselves (in public). Ibsen had jostled our self-satisfaction sadly, but some obliging critic had discovered his formula - a pessimistic decadent - and with consoling verbal bones we worried the old white-haired mastiff of Norway. Only a decadent! It is an easy word to speak in the mouth of the mediocre, and it means nothing. With Nietzsche the case was simpler. We couldn't read him because he was a madman; but he, at least, was an aristocrat who held the bourgeois in contempt, and he also held a brief for culture. Ah! when we are young we are idealists, altruists; as Thackery says, "Youth go to balls; men go to dinners."

But along comes this dreadful Stirner, who cries out: Hypocrites all of you. You are not altruists, but selfish persons, who, self-illuded, believe yourselves to be disinterested. Be Egoists! Confess the truth in the secrecy of your mean, little souls. We are all Egotists. Be Egoists. There is no truth but my truth. No world but my world. I am I. And then Stirner waves away God, state, society, the family, morals, mankind, leaving only the "hateful" ego. The cosmos is frosty and inhuman, and old Mother Earth no longer offers us her bosom as a reclining-place. Stirner has so decreed it. We are suspended between heaven and earth, like Mahomet's coffin hermetically sealed in Self. Instead of "smiting the cord of self," we must reorchestrate the chord that may give out richer music ego.

Nevertheless, there is a magnificent honesty in the words of Max Stirner, that proclaims him to be no vendor of prophylactics. We are weary of the crying in the market-place, "Lo! Christ is risen," only to find an old nostrum tricked out in socialistic phrases; and fine phrases make fine feathers for these gentlemen who offer the millennium in one hand and perfect peace in the other. Stirner is the frankest thinker of his century. He does not soften his propositions, harsh ones for most of us, with promises, but pursues his thought with ferocious logic to its covert. There is no such hybrid with him like "Christian Socialism," no dodging issues. He is a Teutonic Childe Roland who to the dark tower comes, but instead of blowing his horn - as Nietzsche did - he blows up the tower itself. Such an iconoclast has never be fore put pen to paper. He is so sincere in his scorn of all we hold dear that he is refreshing. Nietzsche's flashing epigrammatic blade often snaps after it is fleshed; the grim old Stirner after he makes a jab at his opponent, twists the steel in the wound. Having no mercy for himself, he has no mercy for others. He is never a hypocrit. He erects no altars to known or unknown gods. Humanity, he says, has become the Moloch to-day which every thing is sacrificed. Humanity - that is the State, perhaps, even the Socialistic state (the most awful yoke of all for the individual soul). The assumed love of humanity, this sacrifice of our own personality, are the blights of modern life. The Ego has too long been suppressed by ideas, sacred ideas of religion, state, family, law, morals. The conceptual question, "What is Man?" must be changed to "Who is Man?" I am the owner of my might, and I am so when I know myself as *unique*. What then is my property? Nothing but what is my power. I empower myself. Man is free. *Things* - property - are not. Therefore the State is my enemy, it does not allow me to compete. The poor are to blame for the rich. We should all be the rich. All is for all. I am an owner of property, but property is not sacred. My power is my property; my power give me property; I am myself my own power, and therefore my own property. Stirner is not a communist - so long confounded with anarchs - he does not believe in force. That element came into the world with the advent of Bakounine and Russian nihilism. Stirner would replace society by groups; property would be held, money would be a circulating medium; the present compulsory system would be voluntary instead of involuntary. Unlike his great contemporary, Joseph Proudhon, Stirner is not a constructive philosopher. Indeed, he is no philosopher. A moralist (or immoralist), an *Ethiker*, his book is a defence of Egoism, of the submerged rights of the ego, and in these piping times of peace and fraternal humbug, when every nation, every man embraces his neighbor preparatory to disembowelling him in commerce or war, Max Stirner's words are like a trumpet-blast. And many Jericho-built walls go down before these ringing tones. His doctrine is the Fourth Dimension of ethics. That his book will be more dangerous than a million bombs, if misapprehended, is no reason why it should not be read. Its author can no more be held responsible for its misreading than the orthodox faiths for their backsliders. Nietzsche has been wofully misunderstood; Nietzsche, the despiser of mob

rule, has been acclaimed a very Attila - instead o
which he is a culture-philosopher, one who insist
that reform must be first spiritual. Individualism fo
him means only an end to culture. Stirner is not a
metaphysician; he is too much realist. He is a
Hegelian *á rebours*, a political pyrrhonist. His Ego i
his Categorical Imperative. And if the Individual los
es his value, what is his *raison d'être* for existence
Make your value felt, cries Stirner. The minorit
may occasionally err, but the majority is always i
the wrong. Egoism must not be misinterpreted a
petty selfishness or as an excuse to do wrong. Lif
will be ennobled and sweeter if we respect ou
selves. "There is no sinner and no sinful egoism. .
Do not call men sinful; and *they are not.*" Freedor
is not a goal. "Free - from what? Oh! what is ther
that cannot be shaken off? The yoke of serfdom, c
sovereignty, of aristocracy and princes, the domir
ion of the desires and passions; yes, even the dc
minion of one's own will, of self-will, for the con
pletest self-denial is nothing but freedom - freedon
to wit, from self-determination, from one's own self
This has an ascetic tang, and indicates that to con
pass our complete ego the road travelled will be a
thorny as any saint's of old, Where does Woma
come into this scheme? There is no Woman, only
human Ego. Humanity is a convenient fiction to ha
ry the individualist. So society, family are th
clamps that compress the soul of woman. If woma
is to be free she must first be an individual, an eg
In America, to talk of female suffrage is to propour
the paradox of the masters attacking their slave
yet female suffrage might prove a good thing -
might demonstrate the *reductio ad absurdum* of th
administration of the present ballot system.

A theory needs practical application, just as

religion, worth the name, can exist without dogma (or man without a skeleton). In America, Democracy is on the defensive - it must prove that it is not a failure, that it is not a Boojum that is a Snark; not a Republic that is an Oligarchy. The temper of the people, from Washington to Wall Street, from the Golden Gate to the Bowery, is not for "meddling" reforms, despite the hullabaloo in the press; it rather leans to the methods that will give them something for nothing (power and plunder). All this parade of politics is only the modern substitute for the *panem et circenses* of the old Romans - who, however, were fairer, franker, giving the multitude food and distraction. But for us it is a Barmecide's feast, on paper. In the newspapers we read with tremendous interest about the doings of President this or President that, of the movements and words of Senators and Representatives, as if all this glory and show were aught but a scheme to keep interested - therefore in a not dangerous condition - the people. And these mystifications, intrigues, pothouse politics and high-jinks of the powers that be, do not better economic conditions - for it makes no difference really to the working-man whether Roosevelt or the Mikado is President. Each man is in politics for what it brings *him*. Government by representation only represents the interests of the party or the man who happens to be in the political saddle. The devil take the hindmost! The people go hang! Thus the Stirnerites. Our wail over our neighbor's soul is simply the wail of a busybody. Mind your own business! is the pregnant device of the new Egoism. Puritanism is not morality, but a psychic disorder. Despite the "sweetness and light" diffused by the late Matthew Arnold in England and America, he did not kill, only "scotched" puritanism and philistinism. That it rears its flat, ugly head whenever it dares was demonstrated by the public hysteria over Bernard Shaw, Gorky and the music of Richard Strauss. And then the sweet beast fell upon the choice banquet provided by a notorious murder trial! Of such are your gods, O Philistia. Banish art, banish beauty, but erect an altar, a paper altar, to vulgarity, crime and stupidity. We may have no sense of the eternal verities, but we do possess a pretty and depraved taste in the matter of freak religions.Stirner, in his way, teaches that the Kingdom of God is within you. That man will ever be sufficiently perfected to become his own master is a dreamer's dream. Yet let us dream it. At least by that road we make for righteousness. But let us drop all cant about brotherly love and self sacrifice. Let us love ourselves (respect our ego) that we may learn to respect our brother; self sacrifice means doing something that we believe to be good for our souls, therefore egotism - the higher egotism, withal egotism. As for going to the people - the Russian phrase - let the people forget themselves as a collective body, tribe or group, and each man and woman develop his or her ego. In Russia "going to the people" was sincere - in America it is a trick to catch, not souls, but votes. Our brilliant editorial intellects go down into the mud to spear miserable tadpoles, and after years the mud is as thick, as black as before, the tadpoles more numerous. If sentimental millionaire Socialists could but hear what they are called by the East-Siders who, by the way, are doing most of the thinking this city - they might abandon their self-imposed and charmingly advertised charities.

"The time is not far distant when it will be impossible for any proud, free, independent spirit to ca himself a Socialist, since he would be classed with those wretched toadies and worshippers of success, who even now lie on their knees before every working man and lick his hands simply because he is a working-man." Trade-unionism is become more menacing than the trusts.

John Henry Mackay spoke those truthful words in a striking book of his. Did not Campanella, in an unforgettable sonnet, sing, "The people is a beast of muddy brain that knows not its own strength... With its own hands it ties and gags itself"? Max Stirner may shock, may amuse you. But he is bound to set you thinking.

BLAKE

The Monist

Vol. 21, No. 3 (July 1911), pp. 376-397

"Max Stirner, The Predecessor of Nietzsche" by Paul Carus.

Friedrich Nietzche, the author of *Thus Spake Zarathustra* and the inventor of a new ideal called the "overman," is commonly regarded as the most extreme egotist, to whom morality is non-existent and who glories in the coming of the day in which a man of his liking - the overman - would live *au grand jour*. His philosophy is an individualism carried to its utmost extreme, sanctioning egotism, denouncing altruism and establishing the right of the strong to trample the weak under foot. It is little known, however, that he followed another thinker, Johann Caspar Schmidt, whose extreme individualism he adopted. But this forerunner who preached a philosophy of the sovereignty of self and an utter disregard of our neighbors' rights remained unheeded; he lived in obscurity, he died in poverty, and under the pseudonym "Max Stirner" he left behind a book entitled *Der Einzige und sein Eigentum.*

The historian Lange briefly mentioned him in his *History of Materialism*, and the novelist John Henry Mackay followed up the reference which led to the discovery of this lonely comet on the philosophical sky.

The strangest thing about this remarkable book consists in the many coincidences with Friedrich Ni-

etzsche's philosophy. It is commonly deemed im
possible that the famous spokesman of the over
man should not have been thoroughly familiar with
this failure in the philosophical book market; bu
while Stirner was forgotten the same ideas trans
planted into the volumes of the author of *Thu.
Spake Zarathustra* found an echo first in German
and soon afterwards all over the world.Stirner'
book has been Englished by Stephen T. Byingto
with an introduction by J. L. Walker at the instiga
tion of Benjamin R. Tucker, the representative c
American peaceful anarchism, under the title *Th
Ego and His Own*. They have been helped by M
George Schumm and his wife Mrs. Emma Helle
Schumm. These five persons, all interested in thi
lonely and unique thinker, must have had muc
trouble in translating the German original an
though the final rendering of the title is not inappro
priate, the translator and his advisers agree that
falls short of the mark. For the accepted form Mr. E
R. Tucker is responsible, and he admits in the pre
ace that it is not an exact equivalent of the Germa
Dor Einzige means "the unique man," a person of
definite Individuality, but in the book itself our a
thor modifies and enriches the meaning of the ter
The unique man becomes the ego and an own
(*ein Eigener*), a man who is possessed of propert
especially of his own being. He is a master of h
own and he prides himself on his ownhood, as we
as his ownership. As such he is unique, and th
very term indicates that the thinker who propose
this view-point is an extreme individualist.
Stirner's opinion Christianity pursued the ideal
liberty, liberty from the world; and in this sen
Christians speak of spiritual liberty. To become fr
from anything that oppresses us we must get rid

it, and so the Christian to rid himself of the world becomes a prey to the idea of a contempt of the world. Stirner declares that the future has a better lot in store for man. Man shall not merely be free, which is a purely negative quality, but he shall be his own master; he shall become an owner of his own personality and whatever else he may have to control. His end and aim is he himself. There is no moral duty above him. Stirner explains in the very first sentence of his book:

> What is not supposed to be my concern! First and fore-most, the good cause, then God's cause, the cause of mankind, of truth, of freedom, of humanity, of justice; further, the cause of my people, my prince, my fatherland; finally, even the cause of mind, and a thousand other causes. Only my cause is never to be my concern. 'Shame on the egoist who thinks only of himself!'

Stirner undertakes to refute this satirical explanation in his book on the unique man and his own, and a French critic according to Paul Lauterbach (p. 5) speaks of his book as *un livre qu'on quitte monarque*, "a book which one lays aside a king." Stirner is opposed to all traditional views. He is against church and state. He stands for the self-development of every individual, and insists that the highest duty of every one is to stand up for his own-hood.

J. L. Walker in his Introduction contrasts Stirner with Nietzsche and gives the prize of superiority to the former, declaring him to be a genuine anarchist not less than Josiah Warren, the ideal of the small band of New England anarchists. He says:

In Stirner we have the philosophical foundation for political liberty. His interest in the practical development of egoism to the dissolution of the state and the union of freemen is clear and pronounced, and harmonizes perfectly with the economic philosophy of Josiah Warren. Allowing for difference of temperament and language, there is a substantial agreement between Stirner and Proudhon. Each would be free, and sees in every increase of the number of free people and their intelligence an auxiliary force against the oppressor. But, on the other hand, will any one for a moment seriously contend that Nietzsche and Proudhon march together in general aim and tendency, - that they have anything in common except the daring to profane the shrine and sepulcher of superstition?Nietzsche has been much spoken of as a disciple of Stirner, and, owing to favorable cullings from Nietzsche's writings, it has occurred that one of his books has been supposed to contain more sense than it really does - so long as one had read only the extracts.Nietzche cites scores or hundreds of authors. Had he read everything, and not read Stirner?

But Nietzche is as unlike Stirner as a tight-rope performance is unlike an algebraic equation.Stirner loved liberty for himself, and loved to see any and all men and women taking liberty, and he had no lust for power. Democracy to him was sham liberty, egoism the genuine liberty.Nietzsche, on the contrary, pours out his contempt upon democracy because it is not aristocratic. He is predatory to the point of demanding that those who must succumb to feline rapacity shall be taught to submit with resignation. When he speaks of 'anarchistic dogs' scouring the streets of great civilized cities, it is true, the context shows that he means the communists; but his worship of Napoleon, his bathos of anxiety for the rise of an aristocracy that sh rule Europe for thousands of years, his idea of treating women in the Oriental fashion, show that Nietzsche has struck out in a very old path - doing the apotheosis of tyranny. We individual egoistic anarchists, however, may say to the Nietzsche school, so as not to be misunderstood: We do not ask of the Napoleons to have pity, nor of the predatory barons to do justice. They will find it convenient for their own welfare to make terms with men who have learned of Stirner what a man can be who worships nothing, bears allegiance to nothing. To Nietzsche's rhodomontade of eagles in baronial form, born to prey on industrial lambs, we rather tauntingly oppose the ironical question: Where are your claws? What if the 'eagles' are found to be plain barnyard fowls on which more silly fowls have fastened steel spurs to hack the victims, who, however, have the power to disarm the sham 'eagles' between two suns? Stirner shows that men make their tyrants as they make their gods, and his purpose is to unmake tyrants.Nietzche dearly loves a tyrant.

In style Stirner's work offers the greatest possible contrast to the puerile, padded phraseology of Nietzsche's *Zarathustra* and its false imagery. Who ever imagined such an unnatural conjuncture as an eagle 'toting' a serpent in friendship? which performance is told of in bare words, but nothing comes of it. In Stirner we are treated to an enlivening and earnest discussion addressed to serious minds, and every reader feels that the word is to him, for his instruction and benefit, so far as he has mental independence and courage to take it and use it. The startling intrepidity of this book is infused with a whole-hearted love for all mankind, as evidenced by the fact that the author shows not one iota of prejudice or any idea of division of men into ranks. He would lay aside government, but would establish any regulation deemed convenient, and for this only our convenience is consulted. Thus there will be general liberty only when the disposition toward tyranny is met by intelligent opposition that will no longer submit to such a rule. Beyond this the manly sympathy and philosophical bent of Stirner are such that rulership appears by contrast a

vanity, an infatuation of perverted pride. We know not
whether we more admire our author or more love him.

Stirner's attitude toward woman is not special. She is an in
dividual if she can be, not handicapped by anything h
says, feels, thinks, or plans. This was more fully exempli
fied in his life than even in this book; but there is not a lin
in the book to put or keep woman in an inferior position to
man, neither is there anything of caste or aristocracy in the
book.

It is not our intention to enter here into a detailed
criticism of Stirner's book. We will only point ou
that society will practically remain the sam
whether we con sider social arrangements as vo
untary contracts or as organically developed socia
institutions, or as imposed upon mankind by the d
vine world-order, or even if czars and kings claim t
govern "by the grace of God." Whatever religious c
natural sanction any government may claim to pos
sess, the method of keeping order will be the sam
everywhere. Wrongs have been done and in the fu
ture may still be committed in the name of righ
and injustice may again and again worst justice i
the name of the law. On the other hand, howeve
we can notice a progress throughout the world of
slow but steady improvement of conditions. An
globe-trotter will find by experience that his perso
al safety, his rights and privileges are practically th
same in all civilized countries, whether they are r
publics like Switzerland, France and the Unite
States, or monarchies like Sweden, Germany an
Italy. At the same time murders, robberies, thef
and other crimes are committed all over the worl
even in the homes of those who pride themselve
on being the most civilized nations. The world-co
ception lying behind our different social theories
the same wherever the same kind of civilizatic

prevails. Where social evils prevail, dissatisfaction sets in which produces theories and reform programs, and when they remain unheeded by reaching a certain climax, leads to revolution.Stirner's book begins with a short exhortation headed with Gothe's line,

"My trust in nothingness is placed."

He discusses the character of human life (Chap. I) and contrasts men of the old and the new eras (Chap. II). He finds that the ancients idealized bodily existence while Christianity incarnates the ideal. Greek artists transfigure actual life; in Christianity the divine takes abode in the world of flesh, God becomes incarnate in man. The Greeks tried togo beyond the world and Christianity came; Christian thinkers are pressed to go beyond God, and there they find spirit. They are led to a contempt of the world and will finally end in a contempt of spirit. But Stirner believes that the ideal and the real can never be conciliated, and we must free ourselves from the errors of the past. The truly free man is not the one who has become free, but the one who has come into his own, and this is the sovereign ego.

As Achilles had his Homer so Stirner found his prophet in a German socialist of Scotch Highlander descent, John Henry Mackay. The reading public should know that Mackay belongs to the same type of restless reformers, and he soon became an egoistic anarchist, a disciple of Stirner. His admiration is but a natural consequence of conditions. Nevertheless Mackay's glorification of Stirner proves that i n Stirner this one sided world-conception has found its classical, its most consistent and its philosophically most systematic presentation. Whatever

we may have to criticize in anarchism, Stirner is a
man of uncommon distinction, the leader of a party
and the standard bearer of a cause distinguished
by the extremeness of its propositions which from
the principle of individualism are carried to their
consistent ends. Mackay undertook the difficult task
of unearthing the history of a man who, naturally
modest and retired, had nowhere left deep impres-
sions. No stone remained unturned and every clue
that could reveal anything about his hero's life was
followed up with unprecedented devotion. He published the results of his labors in a book entitled
Max Stirner, His Life and His Work[1]. The report is
extremely touching not so much on account of the
great significance of Stirner's work which to impar-
tial readers appears exaggerated, but through the
personal tragedy of a man who towers high over his
surroundings and suffers in the misery of poverty
and failure.

Mr. Mackay describes Stirner as of medium
height, rather less so than more, well proportioned
slender, always dressed with care though without
pretension, having the appearance of a teacher
and wearing silver- or steel-rimmed spectacles. His
hair and beard were blonde with a tinge of red, his
eyes blue and clear, but neither dreamy nor penetrating. His thin lips usually wore a sarcastic smile
which however had nothing of bitterness; his general appearance was sympathetic. No portrait of
Stirner is in existence except one pencil sketch
which was made from memory in 1892 by the London socialist Friedrich Engels, but the criticism
made by those who knew Stirner that his features,
especially his chin and the top of his head, were not
so angular though nose and mouth are said to have
been well portrayed, and Mackay claims that he

1   *Max Stirner, sein Leben und sein Werk.* Berlin,
Schuster, 1898.

never wore a coat and collar of that type.

BLAKE

Stirner was of purely Frankish blood. His ances
tors lived for centuries in or near Baireuth. His fa
ther, Albert Christian Heinrich Schmidt of Anspach
a maker of wind instruments, died of consumption
in 1807 at the age of 37, a half a year after the birth
of his son. His mother, Sophie née Reinlein of the
city of Erlangen, six months later married H. F. L
Ballerstedt, the assistant in an apothecary shop in
Helmstedt, and moved with him to Kulm on the Vis
tula. In 1818 the boy was sent back to his native
city where his childless god-father and uncle Jo
hann Caspar Martin Sticht and his wife took care of
him.

Young Johann Caspar passed through school
with credit, and his schoolmates used to call him
"Stirner" on account of his high forehead (*Stirn*
which was the most conspicuous feature of his
face. This name clung to him throughout life. In fac
his most intimate friends never called him by an
other, his real name being almost for gotte
through disuse and figuring only in official docu
ments.Stirner attended the universities of Erlange
Berlin and Königsberg, and finally passed his e:
amination for admission as a teacher in gymnasi
schools. His step father died in the summer of 183
in Kulm at the age of 76. It is not known what be
came of his mother who had been mentally u
sound for some time.

Neither father nor stepfather had ever been su
cessful, and if Stirner ever received any inheritanc
it must have been very small. On December 12
1837 Stirner married Agnes Clara Kunigunde Burt
the daughter of his landlady.

Their married life was brief, the young wife dyir

in a premature child-birth on August 29th. We have no indication of an ardent love on either side. He who wrote with passionate fire and with so much insistence in his philosophy, was calm and peaceful, subdued and quiet to a fault in real life.

Having been refused appointment in one of the public or royal schools Stirner accepted a position in a girls' school October 1, 1839. During the political fermentation which preceded the revolutionary year of 1848, he moved in the circle of those bold spirits who called themselves *Die Freien* and met at Hippel's, among whom were Ludwig Buhl, Meyen, Friedrich Engels, Mussak, C. F. Köppenn, the author of a work on Buddha, Dr. Arthur Müller and the brothers Bruno, Egbert and Edgar Bauer. It was probably among their associates that Stirner met Marie Dähnhardt of Gadebusch near Schwerin, Mecklenburg, the daughter of an apothecary, Helmuth Ludwig Dähnhardt. She was as different from Stirner as a dashing emancipated woman can be from a gentle meek man, but these contrasts were joined together in wedlock on October 21, 1843. Their happiness did not last long, for Marie Dähnhardt left her husband at the end of three years.

The marriage ceremony of this strange couple has been described in the newspapers and it is almost the only fact of Stirner's life that stands out boldly as a well-known incident. That these descriptions contain exaggerations and distortions is not improbable, but it cannot be denied that much contained in the reports must be true.

On the morning of October 21, a clergyman of extremely liberal views, Rev. Marot, a member of the Consistory, was called to meet the witnesses of

the ceremony at Stirner's room. Bruno Bauer, Buhl
probably also Julius Faucher, Assessor Kochius
and a young English woman, a friend of the bride
were present. The bride was in her week-day
dress. Mr. Marot asked for a Bible, but none could
be found. According to one version the clergyman
was obliged to request Herr Buhl to put on his coat
and to have the cards removed. When the rings
were to be exchanged the groom discovered that
he had for gotten to procure them, and according to
Wilhelm Jordan's recollection Bauer pulled out his
knitted purse and took off the brass rings, offering
them as a substitute during the ceremony. After the
wedding a dinner with cold punch was served to
which Mr. Marot was invited. But he refused, while
the guests stayed on and the wedding carousal
proceeded in its jolly course.

In order to understand how this incident was
possible we must know that in those pre-revolution
ary years the times were out of joint and these he
roes of the rebellion wished to show their disre
spect and absolute indifference to a ceremony that
to them had lost all its sanctity.Stirner's married life
was very uneventful, except that he wrote the main
book of his life and dedicated it to his wife after
year's marriage, with the words,

Meinem Liebchen

Marie Dähnhardt

Obviously this form which ignores the fact that
they were married, and uses a word of endearment
which in this connection is rather trivial, must be re
garded as characteristic for their relation and their
life principles. Certain it is that she understood or

174

the negative features of her husband's ideals and had no appreciation of the genius that stirred within him. Lauterbach, the editor of the Reclam edition of Stirner's book, comments ironically on this dedication with the Spanish motto *Da Dios almen dras al que no tienemuelas*, "God gives almonds to those who have no teeth."

Marie Dähnhardt was a graceful blonde woman rather under-sized with heavy hair which surrounded her head in ringlets according to the fashion of the time. She was very striking and became a favorite of the round table of the *Freien* who met at Hippel's. She smoked cigars freely and sometimes donned male attire, in order to accompany her husband and his friends on their nightly excursions. It appears that Stirner played the most passive part in these adventures, but true to his principle of individuality we have no knowledge that he ever criticized his wife.

Marie Dähnhardt had lost her father early and was in possession of a small fortune of 10,000 thalers, possibly more. At any rate it was considered quite a sum in the circle of Stirner's friends, but it did not last long. Having written his book, Stirner gave up his position so as to prevent probable discharge and now they looked around for new resources. Though Stirner had studied political economy he was a most unpractical man; but seeing there was a dearth of milk-shops, he and his wife started into business. They made contracts with dairies but did not advertise their shop, and when the milk was delivered to hem they had large quantities of milk on hand but no patrons, the result being a lamentable failure with debts.

In the circle of his friends Stirner's business ex
perience offered inexhaustible material for jokes
while at home it led rapidly to the dissolution of his
marriage. Frau Schmidt complained in later years
that her husband had wasted her property, while no
complaints are known from him. One thing is sure
that they separated. She went to England where
she established herself as a teacher under the pro
tection of Lady Bunsen, the wife of the Prussian
embassador.

Frau Schmidt's later career is quite checkered
She was a well-known character in London. One of
her friends there was a Lieutenant Techow. When
she was again in great distress she emmigrated
with other Germans, probably in 1852 or 1853, to
Melbourne, Australia. Here she tasted the misery of
life to the dregs. She made a living as a washer
woman and is reported to have married a day la
borer. Their bitter experiences made her resort to
religion for consolation, and in 1870 or 1871 she
became a convert to the Catholic Church. At her
sister's death she became her heir and so restored
her good fortune to some extent. She returned
toLondon where Mr. Mackay to his great joy disco
ered that she was still alive at the advanced age of
eighty. What a valuable resource her remini
cences would be for his inquiries! But she refused
to give any information and finally wrote him a letter
which literally reads as follows: "Mary Smith
solemnly avowes that she will have *no more* corre
spondence on the subject, and authorizes M
_____[2] to return all those writings to their own
ers. She is ill and for death."
_____
[2]   The name of the gentleman she mentions is
replaced by a dash at his express wish in the facsimile
her letter reproduced in Mr. Mackay's book (p. 255.)

The last period of Stirner's life, from the time when his wife left him to his death is as obscure as his childhood days. He moved from place to place, and since his income was very irregular creditors pressed him hard. His lot was tolerable because of the simple habits of his life, his only luxury consisting in smoking a good cigar. In 1853 we find him at least twice in debtor's prison, first 21 days, from March 5 to 26, 1853, and then 36 days, from New Year's eve until February 4 of the next year. In the mean time (September 7) he moved to Philipp-strasse 19. It was Stirner's last home. He stayed with the landlady of this place, a kind-hearted woman who treated all her boarders like a mother, until June 25, 1856, when he died rather suddenly as the result of the bite of a poisonous fly. A few of his friends, among them Bruno Bauer and Ludwig Buhl, attended his funeral; a second-class grave was procured for one thaler 10 groats, amounting approximately to one dollar.

During this period Stirner undertook several literary labors from which he possibly procured some remuneration. He translated the classical authors on political economy from the French and from the English, which appeared under the title *Die National-al-Oekonomen der Franzosen und Engländer* (Leipsic: Otto Wigand, 1845-1847).

He also wrote a history of the Reaction which he explained to be a mere counter-revolution. This *Geschichte der Reaction* was planned as a much more comprehensive work, but the two volumes which appeared were only two parts of the second volume as originally intended.

The work is full of quotations, partly from Au-

guste Comte, partly from Edmund Burke. None o
these works represent anything typically original o
of real significance in the history of human thought.

His real contribution to the world's literature re
mains his work *Der Einzige und sein Eigentum*, the
title of which is rendered in English *The Ego and
His Own*, and this, strange to say, enthrones the in
dividual man, the ego, every personality, as a sov
ereign power that is not subject to morality or rules
or obligations, or duties of any kind. The appeal i
made so directly that it will convince all those half
educated and immature minds who after havin
surrendered their traditional faith find themselve
without any authority in either religion or politics
God is to them a fable and the state an abstraction
Ideas and such as truth, goodness, beauty, ar
mere phrases. What then remains but the concret
bodily personality of every man of which every on
is the ultimate standard of right and wrong?

It is strange that neither of these philosophers o
individuality, Nietzsche or Stirner, has ever take
the trouble to investigate what an individual i
Stirner halts before this most momentous questio
of his world-conception, and so he overlooks tha
his ego, his own individuality, this supreme sove
eign standing beyond right and wrong, the ultima
authority of everything, is a hazy, fluctuating, unce
tain thing which differs from day to day and final
disappears.

The individuality of any man is the product
communal life. No one of us could exist as a rati
nal personality were he not a member of a soci
group from which he has imbibed his ideas as we
as his language. Every word is a product of his i

tercourse with his fellow-beings. His entire existence consists in his relations toward others and
finds expression in his attitude toward social institutions. We may criticize existent institutions but we
can never do without any. A denial of either their
existence or their significance proves an utter lack
of in sight into the nature of personality.

We insert here a few characteristic sentences of
Stirner's views, and in order to be fair we follow the
condensation of Mackay (pp. 135-192) than whom
certainly we could find no more sympathetic or intelligent student of this individualistic philosophy.

> Stirner claims the ancients came to the conclusions that
> man was spirit. They created a world of spirit, and in this
> world of spirit Christianity begins. But what is spirit? Spir-
> it has originated from nothing. It is its own creation and
> man makes it the center of the world. The injunction was
> made, thou shalt not live to thyself but to thy spirit, to thy
> ideas. Spirit is the God, the ego and the spirit are in con-
> stant conflict. Spirit dwells beyond the earth. It is in vain to
> force the divine into service here for I am neither God nor
> man, neither the highest being nor my being. The spirit is
> like a ghost whom no one has seen, but of whom there are
> innumerable creditable witnesses, such as grandmother can
> give account of. The whole world that surrounds thee is
> filled with spooks of thy imagination. The holiness of truth
> which hallows thee is a strange element. It is not thine own
> and strangeness is a characteristic of holiness. The specter
> is truly only in thine ownhood... Right is a spleen con-
> ferred by a spook; might, that is myself. I am the mighty
> one and the owner of might... Right is the royal will of so-
> ciety. Every right which exists is created right. I am ex-
> pected to honor it where I find it and subject myself to it.
> But what tome is the right of society, the right of all? What
> do I care for equality of right, for the struggle for right, for
> inalienable rights? Right becomes word in law. The domi-
> nant will is the preserver of the states. My own will shall

upset them. Every state is a despotism. All right and al
power is claimed to belong to the community of the peo
ple. I, however, shall not allow myself to be bound by it
for I recognize no duty even though the state may cal
crime in me what it considers right for itself. My relatio:
to the state is not the relation of one ego to another ego. I
is the relation of the sinner to the saint, but the saint is
mere fixed idea from which crimes originate (Mackay
pages 154-5).

It will sometimes be difficult to translate Stirner'
declarations in their true meaning; for instance:

I am the owner of mankind, I am mankind and shall d
nothing for the benefit of another mankind. The proper
of mankind is mine. I do not respect the property c
mankind. Poverty originates when I can not utilize m
own self as I want to. It is the state which hinders me
from entering into a direct relation with others. On tl
mercy of right my private property depends. Only with
prescribed limits am I allowed to compete. Only the med
um of exchange, the money which the state makes, am
allowed to use. The forms of the state may change, tl
purpose of the state always remains the same. My prope
ty, however, is what I empower myself to. Let violence d
cide, I expect all from my own.

You shall not lure me with love, nor catch me with t
promise of communion of possessions, but the question
property will be solved only through a war of all again
all, and what a slave will do as soon as he has broken h
fetters we shall have to see. I know no law of love. As e
ery one of my sentiments is my property, so also is love
give it, I donate it, I squander it merely because it mak
me happy. Earn it if you believe you have a right to it. T
measure of my sentiments can not be prescribed to me, n
the aim of my feelings determined. We and the world ha
only one relation towards each other, that of usefulne
Yea, I use the world and men. (Pp. 156-157.)

As to promises made and confidence solicited Stirner would not allow a limitation of freedom. He says: "In itself an oath is no more sacred than a lie is contemptible." Stirner opposes the idea of communism. "The community of man creates laws for society. Communism is a communion in equality." Says Stirner, "I prefer to depend on the egotism of men rather than on their compassion." He feels himself swelled into a temporary, transient, puny deity. No man expresses him rightly, no concept defines him; he, the ego, is perfect. Stirner concludes his book: "Owner I am of my own power and I am such only when I know myself as the only one. In the only one even the owner returns into his creative nothingness from which he was born. Any higher being above, be it God or man, detracts from the feeling of my uniqueness and it pales before the sun of this consciousness. If I place my trust in myself, the only one, it will stand upon a transient mortal creator of himself, who feeds upon himself, and I can say,

Ich hab mein Sach' auf nichts gestellt.

In nothingness I placed my trust.

We call attention to Stirner's book, *The Only One and His Ownhood*, not because we are overwhelmed by the profundity of his thought but because we believe that here is a man who ought to be answered, whose world conception deserves a careful analysis which finally would lead to a justification of society, the state and the ideals of right and truth.

Society is not, as Stirner imagines, an artificial product of men who band themselves together in

order to produce a state to the benefit of a clique
Society and state, as well as their foundation the
family, are of a natural growth. All the several social
institutions (kind of spiritual organ isms) are a
much organisms as are plants and animals. The
cooperation of the state with religious, legal, civil
and other institutions, are as much realities as are
individuals, and any one who would undertake t
struggle against them or treat them as nonentities
will be implicated in innumerable struggles.Stirner
is the philosopher of individualism. To him the indi
vidual, this complicated and fluctuant being, is a re
ality, indeed the only true reality, while other combi
nations, institutions and social units are deemed t
be mere nonentities. If from this standpoint the ind
vidualism of Stirner were revised, the student wou!
come to radically different conclusions, and these
conclusions would show that not without good rea
sons has the individual developed as a by-produ
of society, and all the possessions, intellectual a
well as material, which exist are held by individua
only through the assistance and with the permis
sion of the whole society or its dominant factors.

Both socialism and its opposite, individualism
which is ultimately the same as anarchism, are e
tremes that are based upon an erroneous interpre
tation of communal life. Socialists make societ
and anarchists the individual their ultimate princip
of human existence. Both are factors and both fa
tors are needed for preserving the health of socie
as well as comprehending the nature of mankin
By neglecting either of these factors, we can on
be led astray and arrive at wrong conclusions.

Poor Stirner wanted to exalt the ego, the sove
eign individual, not only to the exclusion of a tra

scendent God and of the state or any other power, divine or social, but even to the exclusion of his own ideals, be it truth or anything spiritual; and yet he himself sacrificed his life for a propaganda of the ego as a unique and sovereign being. He died in misery and the recognition of his labors has slowly, very slowly, followed after his death. Yea, even after his death a rival individualist, Friedrich Nietzsche, stole his thunder and reaped the fame which Stirner had earned. Certainly this noble-minded, modest, altruistic egotist was paid in his own coin.

D i d Stirner live up to his principle of ego sovereignty? In one sense he did; he recognized the right of every one to be himself, even when others infringed upon his own well-being. His wife fell out with him but he respected er sovereignty and justified her irregularities. Apparently he said to himself, "She has as much right to her own personality as I to mine." But in another sense so far as he himself was concerned, he did not. What be came of his own rights, his ownhood, and the sweeping claim that the world was his property, that he was entitled to use or misuse the world and all mankind as he saw fit; that no other human being could expect recognition, nay not even on the basis of contracts, or promises, or for the sake of love, or humaneness and compassion? Did Stirner in his poverty ever act on the principle that he was the owner of the world, that there was no tie of morality binding on him, no principle which he had to respect? Nothing of the kind. He lived and died in peace with all the world, and the belief in the great ego sovereignty with its bold renunciation of all morality was a mere Platonic idea, a tame theory which had not the slightest influence upon his practical life.

Men of Stirner's type do not farewell in a world where the ego has come into its own. They will be trampled under foot, they will be bruised and starved, and they will die by the wayside. No, men of Stirner's type had better live in the protective shadow of a state; the worst and most despotic state will be better than none, for no state means mob rule or the tyranny of the bulldozer, the ruffian the brutal and unprincipled self-seeker.

Here Friedrich Nietzsche comes in. Like Nietzsche was a peaceful man; but unlike Stirner, Nietzsche had a hankering for power. Being pathological himself, without energy, without strength and without a healthy appetite and a good stomach, Nietzsche longed to play the part of a bulldozer among a herd of submissive human creatures whom he would control and command. This is Nietzsche's ideal, and he calls it the "overman[3]." Here Nietzsche modified and added his own notion to Stirner's philosophy.Goethe coined the word "overman" (*Uebermensch*) in German and used it in the sense of an awe-inspiring being, almost in the sense of *Unmensch*, a man of might without humanity, whose sentiments are those of Titans, wild and unrestrained like the powers of nature. But the same expression was used in its proper sense about two and a half millenniums ago in ancient China, where at the time of Lao-tze the term *chü jen*, "superior man," or *chün tze*, "superior sage" was in common usage. But the overman or chü jen of Lao-tze, of Confucius and other Chinese sages is not a man of power, not a Napoleon, nor

---

3   The translation "superman" is a solecism, for it is unnecessarily a combination of the Latin *super* and Saxon *man*. Say "superhuman" and "overman" but not "overhuman" nor "superman."

an unprincipled tyrant, not a self-seeker of domineering will, not a man whose ego and its welfare is
his sole and exclusive aim, but a Christlike figure,
who puts his self behind and thus makes his self - a
nobler and better self - come to the front, who does
not retaliate, but returns good for evil[4], a man (as
the Greek sage describes him) who would rather
suffer wrong than commit wrong[5].

This kind of higher man is the very opposite of
Nietzsche's overman, and it is the spirit of this nobler conception of a higher humanity which furnish-
es the best ideas of all the religions of the world, of
Lao-tze's Taoism, of Buddhism and of Christianity.
Stirner in his personal life is animated by it, and,
thinking of the wrongs which the individual frequently suffers in a bureaucratic state through red
tape and unnecessary police interference and other
annoyances, he preaches the right of the individual
and treats the state as non-existent - or rather as a
spook, an error which exists only because our
spleen endows it with life. A careful investigation of
the nature of the state as well as of our personality
would have taught Stirner that both the state and
the individual are realities. The state and society
exist as much as the individuals of which they are
composed[6], and no individual can ignore in his
maxims of life the rules of conduct, the moral principles, or whatever you may call that something

---

4   *Lao-tze's Tao Teh King*, Chaps. 49 and 63.

5   For a collection of Greek quotations on the ethics of
returning good for evil, see *The Open Court*, Vol. XV,
1901, pp 9-12.

6   See the author's *The Nature of the State*, 1894, and
Personality, 1911.

which constitutes the conditions of his existence, o
his physical and social surroundings. The dignit
and divinity of personality does not exclude the sig
nificance of super personalities; indeed the two, su
per personal presences with their moral obligation:
and concrete human persons with their rights and
duties, cooperate with each other and produc
thereby all the higher values of life.Stirner i
onesided but, within the field of his onesided view
consistent. Nietzsche spurns consistency but ac
cepts the field of notions created by Stirner, and
glorying in the same extreme individualism, pro
claims the gospel of that individual who on the ba
sis of Stirner's philosophy would make the best of
disorganized state of society, who by taking upo
himself the functions of the state would utilize th
advantages thus gained for the suppression of hi
fellow beings; and this kind of individual is dignifie
with the title "overman."Nietzsche has been blame
for appropriating Stirner's thoughts and twistin
them out of shape from the self assertion of ever
ego consciousness into the autocracy of the unprir
cipled man of power; but we must concede that th
common rules of literary ethics can not apply to ir
dividualists who deny all and any moral authorit
Why should Nietzsche give credit to the author fro
whom he drew his inspiration if neither acknow
edges any rule which he feels obliged to observe
Nietzsche uses Stirner as Stirner declares that it
the good right of every ego to use his fellows, ar
Nietzsche shows us what the result would be - th
rise of a political boss, a brute inhuman shape, th
overman.Nietzsche is a poet, not a philosopher, n
even a thinker, but as a poet he exercises a pec
liar fascination upon many people who would nev
think of agreeing with him. Most admirers of Nie

zsche belong to the class which Nietzsche calls the "herd animals," people who have no chance of ever asserting themselves, and become hungry for power as a sick man longs for health.

Individualism and anarchism continue to denounce the state, where they ought to reform it and improve its institutions. In the mean time the world wags on. The state exists, society exists, and innumerable social institutions exist. The individual grows under the influence of other individuals, his ideas - mere spooks of his brain - yet the factors of his life, right or wrong, guide him and determine his fate. There are as rare exceptions a few lawless societies in the wild West where a few outlaws meet by chance, revolver in hand, but even among them the state of anarchy does not last long, for by habit and precedent certain rules are established, and wherever man meets man, wherever they offer and accept one another's help, they cooperate or compete, they join hands or fight, they make contracts, they cooperate, and establish rules and the result is society, the state, and all the institutions of the state, a government, the legislation, the judiciary and all the intricate machinery which regulates the interrelations of man to man.

BLAKE

INDEX

BLAKE

Books

BLAKE

Names

Periodicals

Allgemeinheit und Einheit des Sittlichen Bewusstseins.........1

American Economic Review, The..12

American Journal of Psychology, The...........................48, 10

American Journal of Semitic Languages and Literatures, The
....2

American Journal of Sociology.....................................18, 6

American Journal of Theology, The................................93, 9

American Magazine of Art, The...12

American Political Science Review, The............................12

Annals of the American Academy of Political and Social
Science..36, 6

Archiv für die gesamte Psychologie.....................................10

Archiv für Rechts- und Wirtschaftsphilosophie...................11

Athenaeum, The..7

Berdiayev, N..10

Books Abroad...12

Chicago Public..

Day Book, The...90

Der Eigene...

Der Geist der neueren Philosophie...

Eagle and the Serpent, The...
....................20pp., 25p., 27, 29p., 30, 34pp., 95pp., 109, 1

Economic Bulletin, The..

Egoist, The...............................80, 82, 84, 87pp., 95p., 98, 1

English Historical Review, The...

Freewoman, The..70,

Giornale degli Economisti, Serie Seconda..............................

Harvard Theological Review, The...1

Hispania..1

Historische Zeitschrift.............................37, 120, 133, 1

Historischen Zeitschrift teilt Bibliotheksrat..........................1

International Journal of Ethics.....................24, 59, 121, 1

Jahrbücher für Nationalökonomie und Statistik...104, 112, 1

Jewish Social Studies...1

Journal of Economics and Statistics.................104, 112, 1

Journal of English and Germanic Philology, The...................

Journal of Institutional and Theoretical Economics.............1

Journal of Philosophy Psychology & Scientific Methods, The
....85pp.,

Journal of Philosophy, The...1

Journal of Political Economy...

Journal of Politics, The...13

Printed in Great Britain
by Amazon

65039879R00124